THE IMPORTANCE OF

John F. Kennedy

These and other titles are included in The Importance Of biography series:

Alexander the Great
Muhammad Ali
Louis Armstrong
James Baldwin
Clara Barton
The Beatles
Napoleon Bonaparte
Julius Caesar
Rachel Carson
Charlie Chaplin
Charlemagne
Cesar Chavez
Winston Churchill
Cleopatra
Christopher Columbus
Hernando Cortes
Marie Curie
Charles Dickens
Emily Dickinson
Amelia Earhart
Thomas Edison
Albert Einstein
Duke Ellington
Dian Fossey
Anne Frank
Benjamin Franklin
Galileo Galilei
Emma Goldman
Jane Goodall
Martha Graham
Lorraine Hansberry
Stephen Hawking
Ernest Hemingway
Jim Henson
Adolf Hitler

Harry Houdini
Thomas Jefferson
Mother Jones
Chief Joseph
John F. Kennedy
Martin Luther King Jr.
Joe Louis
Malcolm X
Thurgood Marshall
Margaret Mead
Golda Meir
Michelangelo
Wolfgang Amadeus Mozart
John Muir
Sir Isaac Newton
Richard M. Nixon
Georgia O'Keeffe
Louis Pasteur
Pablo Picasso
Elvis Presley
Jackie Robinson
Norman Rockwell
Eleanor Roosevelt
Anwar Sadat
Margaret Sanger
Oskar Schindler
William Shakespeare
John Steinbeck
Tecumseh
Jim Thorpe
Mark Twain
Queen Victoria
Pancho Villa
H. G. Wells

John F. Kennedy

by
Michael V. Uschan

Lucent Books, P.O. Box 289011, San Diego, CA 92198-9011

To my father, who was proud to vote for John F. Kennedy in 1960

Library of Congress Cataloging-in-Publication Data

Uschan, Michael V., 1948–
    The importance of John F. Kennedy / by Michael V. Uschan.
        p.   cm. — (The importance of series)
    Includes bibliographical references (p.   ) and index.
    Summary: A biography of the thirty-fifth president of the
United States who served from 1961 until his assassination in
1963.
    ISBN 1-56006-482-X (lib. : alk. paper)
    1. Kennedy, John F. (John Fitzgerald), 1917–1963—Juvenile
literature.   2. Presidents—United States—Biography—Juvenile
literature.   3. United States—Politics and government—1961–
1963—Juvenile literature.   [1. Kennedy, John F. (John Fitzgerald), 1917–1963.   2. Presidents.]   I. Title.   II. Series: Importance of.
E842.Z9U73   1999
973.922'092—dc21   98–36402
    [B]   CIP
                                                              AC

Copyright 1999 by Lucent Books, Inc., P.O. Box 289011,
San Diego, California, 92198-9011

Printed in the U.S.A.

Contents

Foreword   **7**

Important Dates in the Life of John F. Kennedy   **8**

INTRODUCTION
A Life of Triumph and Tragedy   **10**

CHAPTER 1
Growing Up a Kennedy   **13**

CHAPTER 2
JFK: Author, War Hero   **24**

CHAPTER 3
JFK Goes to Washington   **33**

CHAPTER 4
Senator Kennedy: Success, Love, Pain   **41**

CHAPTER 5
JFK: The New Frontier   **52**

CHAPTER 6
JFK and the Challenge of Communism   **63**

CHAPTER 7
Other Challenges: Civil Rights, Space, the Economy   **77**

CHAPTER 8
Dallas: A Fateful Day in History   **91**

EPILOGUE
The Darkness and the Light   **103**

Notes   **106**

For Further Reading   **110**

Works Consulted   **112**

Index   **115**

Picture Credits   **120**

About the Author   **120**

Foreword

THE IMPORTANCE OF biography series deals with individuals who have made a unique contribution to history. The editors of the series have deliberately chosen to cast a wide net and include people from all fields of endeavor. Individuals from politics, music, art, literature, philosophy, science, sports, and religion are all represented. In addition, the editors did not restrict the series to individuals whose accomplishments have helped change the course of history. Of necessity, this criterion would have eliminated many whose contribution was great, though limited. Charles Darwin, for example, was responsible for radically altering the scientific view of the natural history of the world. His achievements continue to impact the study of science today. Others, such as Chief Joseph of the Nez Percé, played a pivotal role in the history of their own people. While Joseph's influence does not extend much beyond the Nez Percé, his nonviolent resistance to white expansion and his continuing role in protecting his tribe and his homeland remain an inspiration to all.

These biographies are more than factual chronicles. Each volume attempts to emphasize an individual's contributions both in his or her own time and for posterity. For example, the voyages of Christopher Columbus opened the way to European colonization of the New World. Unquestionably, his encounter with the New World brought monumental changes to both Europe and the Americas in his day. Today, however, the broader impact of Columbus's voyages is being critically scrutinized. *Christopher Columbus,* as well as every biography in The Importance Of series, includes and evaluates the most recent scholarship available on each subject.

Each author includes a wide variety of primary and secondary source quotations to document and substantiate his or her work. All quotes are footnoted to show readers exactly how and where biographers derive their information, as well as provide stepping-stones to further research. These quotations enliven the text by giving readers eyewitness views of the life and times of each individual covered in The Importance Of series.

Finally, each volume is enhanced by photographs, bibliographies, chronologies, and comprehensive indexes. For both the casual reader and the student engaged in research, The Importance Of biographies will be a fascinating adventure into the lives of people who have helped shape humanity's past and present, and who will continue to shape its future.

IMPORTANT DATES IN THE LIFE OF JOHN F. KENNEDY

1917
The United States enters World War I on April 6; John Fitzgerald Kennedy is born on May 29.

1933
Franklin Delano Roosevelt is sworn in as the thirty-second president of the United States on March 4.

1934
Joseph P. Kennedy becomes the first chairman of the Securities and Exchange Commission on July 2.

1935
John F. Kennedy graduates from Choate.

1938
Joseph Kennedy is appointed ambassador to Great Britain on January 5.

1939
Germany invades Poland on September 1, starting World War II.

1940
John Kennedy graduates from Harvard cum laude on June 20; his honors thesis earns magna cum laude. On August 1, Kennedy's *Why England Slept* is pub-lished. He is appointed an ensign in the naval reserve on October 8. Joseph Kennedy resigns as ambassador to England on December 2.

1941
The United States enters World War II on December 8, one day after Pearl Harbor is attacked.

1943
PT 109 is sunk by a Japanese destroyer on August 2.

1946
On June 18 Kennedy defeats nine other candidates in the Democratic primary for the Eleventh Congressional District; he wins the general election for Congress on November 5.

1950
The Korean War begins on June 25.

1952
On November 4, Kennedy defeats incumbent Henry Cabot Lodge Jr. for a Senate seat.

1953
Kennedy marries Jacqueline Lee Bouvier on September 12.

1956

Kennedy's *Profiles in Courage* is published on January 1; Kennedy loses his bid for the vice presidential nomination at the Democratic convention on August 17.

1957

Profiles in Courage wins the Pulitzer Prize for biography on May 6; the Soviet Union launches *Sputnik I,* the first artificial satellite in space.

1960

Kennedy is elected president of the United States on November 8.

1961

Kennedy is inaugurated as the nation's thirty-fifth president on January 20; on March 1 signs an executive order creating the Peace Corps; on March 13 proposes the long-term Alliance for Progress between the United States and Latin America; assumes responsibility for failed Bay of Pigs invasion on April 20; on May 25 proposes putting an American space team on the moon within the decade; opens Vienna summit on June 3 with Nikita Khrushchev of the Soviet Union; on July 25 reaffirms U.S. commitment to West Berlin and asks Congress for more funds to expand military might and manpower.

1962

Kennedy announces on September 30 that the federal government will carry out the court order admitting James Meredith to the University of Mississippi; on October 22 announces a naval quarantine to halt the Soviet missile buildup in Cuba; Khrushchev subsequently withdraws missiles under U.S. inspection.

1963

Kennedy calls for massive tax reduction and tax reform to help the economy; in a speech at American University on June 10, Kennedy proposes new talks on a nuclear arms test ban treaty; mobilizes the Alabama National Guard on June 11 to admit two black students to the University of Alabama as ordered by the court; proposes the most sweeping civil rights legislation in history on June 22; signs the Limited Nuclear Test Ban Treaty on October 7, the first disarmament agreement of the nuclear age and first sign of a thaw in the Cold War; is assassinated in Dallas on November 22.

A Life of Triumph and Tragedy

John Fitzgerald Kennedy, the youngest person ever elected president of the United States, was sworn in January 20, 1961. The forty-three-year-old Kennedy would serve his nation only 1,036 days. His presidency ended tragically on November 22, 1963, in Dallas, Texas, when he was shot and killed. The assassination abruptly ended a presidency that spanned one of the most dramatic, challenging, and dangerous periods in American history.

While Kennedy was president, the Cold War with the Soviet Union, which had festered poisonously since the end of World War II, brought the two superpowers to the brink of nuclear war over Cuba. The civil rights movement, which had gained strength during the 1950s, exploded into violence in southern states as blacks demanded rights that most Americans took for granted. Communism's worldwide threat to democracy created crises from Southeast Asia to Latin America. At home, a faltering economy and other problems bedeviled Americans.

Leading the nation through this precarious period was a man many Americans had barely known before the 1960 presidential election, a senator from Massachusetts who had defied the odds and political tradition to boldly seize the Democratic nomination from older, better-known rivals.

Most Americans knew only a handful of facts about their new chief executive: Kennedy was the first Roman Catholic to be elected president, he came from a wealthy family with humble roots in Ireland, he was a World War II hero, and he had served in Congress since 1947. Few were aware that he had authored *Profiles in Courage,* which won a Pulitzer Prize for biography, and was the son of Joseph P. Kennedy, the multimillionaire businessman who had been the first chairman of the Securities and Exchange Commission and an ambassador to Great Britain.

Style over Substance

The manner in which people had developed their understanding of who Kennedy was went beyond such simple facts, however. Every American had experienced an emotional reaction to him based on the image he projected on television.

Pictures that flickered on TV screens in homes across America during the 1960 campaign showed a handsome, vigorous young man, whose eloquent speech was tinged by a thick Boston accent that turned *Cuba* into *Cuber* and *vigor,* a favorite word, into *vigah.* In a triumph of style and image over substance, Kennedy was able to establish an electronic rapport with millions of Americans, much to the dismay of his Republican opponent, Richard M. Nixon.

But it is precisely this question of style over substance that makes it so difficult to truly understand Kennedy. Even Charles Bartlett, a journalist in Washington, D.C., and longtime friend of the nation's thirty-fifth president, once said, "No one ever knew John Kennedy, not all of him."[1]

Who Was Kennedy?

Even before assassination elevated his presidency to legendary status, John F. Kennedy had succeeded in wrapping himself and his family in a shroud of myth and mystique that blurred the outlines of who he *really* was.

Although Kennedy appeared to be strong and healthy, an image nurtured by

President John F. Kennedy applauds his mother, Rose, at the 1962 Kennedy Foundation Dinner. Although Rose was portrayed by the media as a loving mother, Kennedy as an adult complained that while he was growing up she was often away from home on trips to Europe or working on various church projects.

TV footage of the Kennedy clan's manic touch football games, he suffered from a variety of serious medical problems. In addition to surviving a series of near-fatal illnesses from childhood into adult life, Kennedy had Addison's disease, which made him highly susceptible to infection; he wore glasses, had allergies, suffered from ulcers, and lived daily with intense back pain that forced him at times to hobble around on crutches, even while he was president.

His younger brother Robert once said: "At least one half of the days that he spent on earth were days of intense physical pain. He had almost every conceivable ailment. When we were growing up we used to laugh about the great risk a mosquito took in biting Jack Kennedy—with some of his blood the mosquito was almost sure to die."[2]

Although Kennedy was able to morally uplift the nation with a soaring inaugural speech in which he called on Americans to "ask not what your country can do for you—ask what you can do for your country,"[3] the public learned years after his death that he had repeatedly broken his marriage vows by having sexual relations with other women, conduct he continued even after being elected president.

While Kennedy was known for his compassion for the poor and for championing the civil rights of African Americans, his social concern was at times guided more by political instincts than moral considerations.

The Kennedy Myth

Some of the misconceptions Americans had about Kennedy—and may have yet today—were due to the normal distortion of learning about a person secondhand, whether the information and impressions come from the mass media or from other people.

But Kennedy, even more than most politicians, worked hard not only to create a certain public image but to actually reshape and color his past for political advantage. He was aided and abetted in this endeavor by members of his family; numerous powerful, articulate friends; and members of the media, some who knew the truth, some who did not.

The misconceptions on which the myth is based cover several areas, including Kennedy's supposedly excellent health; the lives of his family members, in particular his retarded sister, Rosemary; stories of how he joined the navy and entered politics; and the authorship of *Profiles in Courage.*

1 Growing Up a Kennedy

Being a Kennedy shaped John F. Kennedy from the day of his birth. Thus, to understand the man, it is necessary to first understand his family.

John Fitzgerald Kennedy was born in the Boston suburb of Brookline, Massachusetts, on May 29, 1917, shortly after the United States entered World War I. His

John F. Kennedy as an infant in 1918. He was the second child of Joseph P. and Rose Fitzgerald Kennedy.

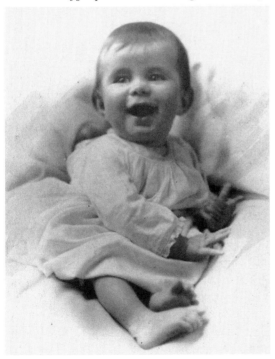

parents were Joseph P. Kennedy, a young man well on his way to fulfilling his goal of becoming a millionaire by age thirty-five, and Rose Fitzgerald, whose father was mayor of Boston for many years.

John F. Kennedy's great-grandfathers were among the thousands of Irish immigrants who came to Boston in the mid–nineteenth century during the potato famine. Pat Kennedy, for example, arrived in the late 1840s and began working as a cooper making barrels. The Irish were looked down on and discriminated against when they first arrived. Biographer James MacGregor Burns describes the life of Irish immigrants during this period:

> About the time Pat Kennedy came to Boston, hundreds of basements housed five to fifteen persons each, with at least one holding thirty-nine every night. One sink might serve a house, one privy [a primitive toilet] a neighborhood. Filth spread through courts and alleys, and with it tuberculosis, cholera, and smallpox, which thrived most in the poorest districts where the Irish lived. The Irish were the lowest of the low, lower than the Germans or the Scandinavians, or even the Negroes, who had come earlier and edged a bit up the economic ladder. Irish men were

The Kennedy children pose in bathing suits in 1928 at the family's summer home in Hyannis Port, Massachusetts. Lined from oldest to youngest (from right to left) are Joseph Jr., Jack, Rosemary, Kathleen, Eunice, Patricia, Robert, and Jean. Edward, called Ted, was not born until 1932.

lucky if they could find part-time work on the dock or in the ditch; Irish girls hoped at best to get work as maids in hotels or in big houses on Beacon Hill. The only defense the Irish had was the classic weapon of oppressed people—solidarity. Tighter and tighter they bound themselves with the throngs of their national identity.[4]

In 1858, a year before he died of cholera, Pat Kennedy and his wife gave birth to a son—Patrick Joseph Kennedy, who became known as P. J. The young widow raised her son and three daughters in poverty, and that son, after only a few years of schooling, went to work on the docks. P. J. saved his money, bought a saloon, branched out into retail liquor sales, and became prosperous.

In Boston in the late 1880s and 1890s the key to salvation for Irish immigrants

was politics. Their increasing numbers and solidarity gave them power, and P. J. became a local boss in the Democratic Party. Another rising Irish politician was John F. "Honey Fitz" Fitzgerald, John F. Kennedy's maternal grandfather.

Although Kennedy and Fitzgerald sometimes clashed in local political battles, they eventually became good friends. In October 1914 the two families were united when Joseph P. Kennedy, P. J.'s son, married Rose Fitzgerald. It was a royal wedding, Irish political style, because Rose's father was Boston's mayor. The ceremony was performed not by a parish priest but by Cardinal William O'Connell.

Jack, as John F. Kennedy was called, was the second of nine Kennedy children. Joseph Kennedy Jr. was born in 1915 and Jack two years later, followed by Rosemary, Kathleen, Eunice, Patricia, Robert, Jean, and Edward, who was called Ted. The Kennedy children lived in style because their father had made good on his promise to become a millionaire.

Kennedy

Joseph Kennedy was born with an insatiable urge to make money. Even though his father was well-off, at the age of eight he began selling peanuts and candy on Boston excursion boats. While attending Harvard, he and a classmate bought a bus for six hundred dollars and operated a sight-seeing business; when they graduated in 1912, they split a profit of ten thousand dollars. Kennedy's first job was as a state bank ex-

Joseph P. Kennedy dedicated his life to making money. A millionaire, he was able to provide the future president and his siblings a lavish lifestyle.

aminer, and in 1913 he became president of Columbia Trust Company after helping the bank defeat a hostile takeover.

Joseph boasted that at age twenty-five he was the youngest bank president in the nation. There is some doubt whether that was true, but he repeated the story so often that it became gospel. Over the years the Kennedys would create other myths about their lives, either to embellish their family history or cover up negatives. For example, the family denied for many years that Rosemary was retarded, and Jack lied repeatedly to conceal the true extent of the medical problems that plagued him his entire life.

Another Kennedy trait was family loyalty. Joseph Kennedy got his first job as a bank examiner because of his father's political connections, and the bank he became president of was partly owned by his father. In 1961, when President Kennedy appointed his brother Robert attorney general, there were cries of protest. But Robert performed admirably and courageously in a difficult period.

During World War I, the senior Kennedy managed Bethlehem Steel's huge shipyard in Quincy, Massachusetts. He earned twenty thousand dollars a year, a huge salary for the time, while breaking production records to make ships that were badly needed to ferry war supplies to Europe. Always alert for any opportunity to make money, Kennedy opened a lunchroom and sold meals to the twenty-two thousand shipyard workers he bossed.

After the war Kennedy threw himself completely into becoming rich. A savvy, versatile businessman, Kennedy made huge sums in the stock market, motion pictures, liquor distribution after the repeal of Prohibition in 1933, and buying and selling real estate. (Some people claim Kennedy also made money by illegally selling liquor during Prohibition.) He amassed a fortune of between $200 and $300 million and established trust funds that made his children millionaires while they were still very young.

The Kennedy Home

The Kennedys moved to Bronxville, New York, when Jack was ten because his father was selling stocks and engaged in other financial ventures in New York City. They also left Boston because, despite their wealth and prominence, the Irish, Roman Catholic Kennedys had never been accepted socially by the city's elite, who were mainly of English descent and were Protestant. The family also had a summer home in Hyannis Port on Cape Cod and a winter home in Palm Beach, Florida. The summer home later became Jack's presidential retreat.

Although Joseph Kennedy liked to boast that "the measure of a man's success in life is not the money he's made, it's the kind of family's he's raised,"[5] he was away from home for weeks at a time while working. While absent, Kennedy also pursued women; his unfaithfulness to his marriage vows was a trait he passed on to his second son. Rose tried to escape the grief caused by her husband's behavior by making fre-

Joseph Jr. (left) and Jack at Hyannis Port, Massachusetts in 1925. Although Joe became a surrogate father to his siblings because their parents were absent so much, he and Jack were bitter rivals who constantly tried to top each other in athletics, academics, and other pursuits.

quent trips to Europe to buy clothes and spending many hours doing charitable deeds and church work. Thus, during Jack's childhood there were many times when neither parent was home.

As an adult John F. Kennedy made conflicting statements about his mother. He once said: "She was terribly religious. She was a little removed, and still is, which I think is the only way to survive when you have nine children. I thought she was a very model mother for a big family."[6] But another time, in a more bitter mood, Kennedy stated: "My mother was either at some Paris fashion house or else on her knees in some church. She was never there when we really needed her. My mother never really held me and hugged me. Never! Never!"[7]

In her autobiography, Rose cites the amount of time that she had to devote to her daughter Rosemary as justification for failing to give her other children enough attention.

Even when absent, however, Jack's father was interested in his children, constantly writing letters and calling them. When he was home, the dinner table became a proving ground for his children, who were required to read news stories from a bulletin board and discuss current events during meals. Joseph Kennedy usually spent more time questioning and lecturing his children than conversing about family matters.

Competition was a vital part of life for Kennedy children, and only one position counted—first place. Burns describes the competitive crucible that shaped the future president's appetite for winning:

The father wanted his children to be competitive with one another, and they vied among themselves fiercely in par-

Rose Fitzgerald in 1911. This mother of a future president grew up in a political atmosphere. Her father was mayor of Boston when she married Joseph P. Kennedy.

lor games and sports. Sometimes the girls would leave the tennis courts in tears after being bested by their brothers. Touch football games were almost fratricidal. "They are the most competitive and at the same time the most cohesive family I've ever seen," said a longtime family friend some years after. "They fight each other, yet they feed on each other. They stimulate each other. Their minds strike sparks. Each of them has warm friends but none they like and admire so much as they like and admire their own brothers and sisters." [Joe] wanted his children, however competitive they might be with one another, to present a united front against the outside world.[8]

Jack's Allowance

Even as a young boy John Kennedy could argue forcefully and articulately for what he wanted. In an example quoted by James MacGregor Burns in John Kennedy, A Political Profile, *the future president, age ten, shows his budding persuasive powers in this formal, written request to his father for a raise in allowance.*

"My recent allowance is 40¢. This is used for aeroplanes and other playthings of childhood but now I am a scout and I put away my childish things. Before I would spend 20¢ of my 40¢ allowance and in five minutes I would have empty pockets and nothing to gain and 20¢ to lose. When I am a scout I have to buy canteens, haversacks, blankets, searchlicgs [sic], poncho things that will last for years and I can always use it while I can't use chocolate marshmallow sunday [sic] ice cream and so I put in my plea for a raise of thirty cents for me to buy schut [sic] things and pay my own way around."

As comical as it may seem for a millionaire's son to argue for an extra thirty cents a week, Burns notes that there was "no record of the effect of the petition on his father." As the errors in the note indicate, Kennedy was a poor speller, a disability he never conquered.

Young John F. Kennedy poses for the camera while dressed in a policeman's costume. The photo was taken in Brookline, Massachusetts, in either 1925 or 1926.

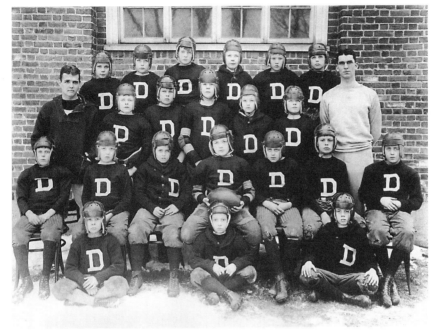

Nine-year-old Jack Kennedy (seated on the ground, far right) was a member of the 1926 Dexter Academy football team in Brookline, Massachusetts. One row above him (third from the left) is his older brother Joe. Sports were an important part of life for the Kennedy children.

With both parents absent much of the time, Joe Jr. became a surrogate parent, protecting his siblings and teaching them to sail and swim. But he could also be mean and bully them. He and Jack had a bitter rivalry—which their mother called a "friendly enmity"[9]—that once resulted in Jack needing twenty-eight stitches. The brothers had set out in opposite directions in a race around the block on their bicycles; they collided head-on when neither would give way as they approached the finish line.

Childhood Illnesses

Receiving medical attention was nothing new for Jack, who had scarlet fever, whooping cough, measles, and chicken pox before he was three. When he was hospitalized for several months in early 1920 with scarlet fever, Jack was given last rites by a priest, an act performed only when death appears imminent. It was the first of many times he would receive this sacrament of his church.

Like Theodore Roosevelt, another president who was ill as a child, Kennedy fell in love with books. Even when young, Jack liked history, but he also devoured childhood classics such as *King Arthur and His Knights* and *The Arabian Nights*. Rose once said that "as a child and many times thereafter he had to spend long periods in bed . . . and as a consequence he learned to love to read, and always did read much more than any of the others."[10]

Kennedy also had back problems from an early age. Amazingly, however, these ailments did not hinder young Jack from pursuing sports with wild abandon.

In 1930, at age thirteen, he left home to attend Canterbury School in Milford, Connecticut. But illness accompanied him, and an appendicitis attack that spring

Covering Up His Illnesses

In President Kennedy: Profile of Power, *Richard Reeves comments on Kennedy's penchant for lying about his many physical ailments.*

"There was a gallantry to Kennedy's consistent lying about his health and his success in persuading press and public that he was a man of great energy. 'Vigor' was the cliché used by the press. In truth, boy and man, he was sick and in pain much of the time, often using crutches or a cane in private to rest his back, and taking medication, prescribed and unprescribed, each day, sometimes every hour. He had trouble fighting off ordinary infections and suffered recurrent fevers that raged as high as 106 degrees.

As candidate and president, Kennedy concealed his low energy level, radiating health and good humor, though he usually spent more than half of most days in bed. He retired early most nights, read in bed until 9 a.m. or so each morning, and napped an hour each afternoon. Besides all that, Kennedy had persistent venereal [sexually transmitted] disease, a very uncertain stomach that restricted him to a bland diet all his life, some deafness in his right ear, and a baffling range of allergies that sometimes laid him out.

Joining the Navy, he had lied about the fevers and his debilitating back problem, and had somehow managed to get in without a physical examination. In politics, the spinal problems he had suffered since childhood became 'old football injuries' or 'war injuries' and the fierce fevers he had suffered all his life became malaria from the war."

forced him to miss the rest of the school year. That was also the year a doctor first prescribed glasses. For the rest of his life, Kennedy kept this weakness hidden from the public, refusing to be photographed while wearing glasses. That fall he went to Choate, a prestigious prep school in Wallingford, Connecticut, already attended by his brother Joe.

Choate and Harvard

Choate seemed an unusual choice for the Kennedys. For decades the expensive private school had been the training ground for wealthy New England families. But Joseph Kennedy, still angry about being snubbed by elite Boston society, was determined that his sons would have an educa-tion to rival that of the snootiest Boston Brahmin. So he sent his sons to Choate and then to Harvard. His daughters, how-ever, attended Catholic schools.

Jack Kennedy participated in football, baseball, basketball, crew, and golf. He was a lackluster student and was involved in many juvenile pranks with his friends K. LeMoyne "Lem" Billings and Ralph "Rip" Horton, who helped him form the "Muck-ers Club." Members of this informal, secret club dedicated themselves to having fun, playing pranks, and engaging in other mis-chievous behavior. In June 1935 he gradu-ated 65th out of 110 students.

Although Kennedy was content to set-tle for what were called "gentleman's C's," his grades were partly due to boredom with his classes. He read the *New York Times* daily to stay current on world affairs, un-usual for a teenager, and he excelled in history, his favorite subject. His constant illnesses left him terribly skinny, and he looked sickly despite his athletic pursuits. His nickname was "Ratface."

The summer after graduating from Choate, Kennedy went to England to at-tend the London School of Economics, but illness struck again. He became ill with what was diagnosed as either hepatitis or jaundice, and a few weeks later he returned

Jack Kennedy, jauntily holding a cane, and three friends at Choate School who were all members of the Muckers Club, an informal group dedicated to having fun. From left to right are Ralph "Rip" Horton, LeMoyne "Lem" Billings, Charles "Butch" Schriber, and Jack, who was nicknamed "Ratface."

home. He entered Princeton that fall but again became ill and withdrew.

The ailments Kennedy suffered as a youth had a common thread—his susceptibility to colds and other infections. As an adult he was diagnosed with Addison's disease, which is caused by an insufficient secretion of hormones from the adrenal glands. Symptoms of Addison's are weakness, loss of weight, low blood pressure, gastrointestinal problems, and a brownish coloring of the skin. Kennedy stayed tan throughout the year to cover this complexion blemish.

The next year Jack joined his older brother at Harvard. Once again he majored in high jinks and athletics, including football and swimming, his favorite sport. The almost frail-looking would-be athlete was known more for his fierce competitive nature than strength or natural ability. He also discovered the opposite sex and wrote his friend Lem Billings that he was becoming known as a playboy.

The skinny six-footer, who weighed only about 150 pounds, was injured as a sophomore while playing football. Biographer Herbert S. Parmet recounts the incident: "Jack scrimmaged in practice against the much heavier varsity squad and was thrown to the ground. Landing at a bad angle, he ruptured a spinal disc . . . [and] his back became a permanent memento of [his] Harvard days."[11]

But Thomas C. Reeves, in *A Question of Character: A Life of John F. Kennedy,* says the injury was not the real source of Kennedy's lifelong back problems:

Jack was born with what a family physician later called an "unstable back." [Later stories about heroic football and wartime back injuries were largely ficti-

tious.] This slight deformity restricted his activities and, in later life, would cause often acute pain that would last weeks. Rest, hot baths, crutches, and a back brace that looked like a corset were [all prescribed by physicians].[12]

The football injury and the stress to his back during World War II undoubtedly aggravated any back problems already present, but when Kennedy entered political life in 1946, he claimed they were the *only* reasons for his bad back. Those explanations, which somehow seemed more manly, were among the earliest components of the Kennedy mythology.

Kennedy improved as a student in his last two years at Harvard, partly because a long trip to Europe in the summer of 1937 fired his interest in current world affairs. "I guess it was during my sophomore year that I really found myself," Kennedy said. "I don't know what to attribute it to. No, not to my professors. I guess I was just getting older. It was during my junior year that I went to England for six months, which meant taking six courses as a senior and hard work. I had to work like hell."[13]

In January 1938 Kennedy's father was rewarded for services to the Democratic Party by being appointed ambassador to Great Britain, a great coup because of his Irish heritage and a goal he had long sought. He had become an important force behind the scenes in politics, helping Franklin D. Roosevelt win the presidential elections of 1932 and 1936. The ambassadorship as well as two previous federal appointments—as first head of the Securities and Exchange Commission in 1934 and chairman of the U.S. Maritime Commission in 1937—were tokens of gratitude.

A Bad Report from Choate

Although he was bright and showed signs of intellectual and academic ability, John F. Kennedy was a disinterested student in his early years. In Triumph and Tragedy: The Story of the Kennedys, *Sidney C. Moody Jr. includes this letter to Kennedy's father from Seymour St. John, headmaster at Choate.*

"I would be willing to bet anything that within two years you will be as proud of Jack as you are now of [his brother] Joe. Jack has a clever, individualist mind. It is a harder mind to put in harness than Joe's—harder for Jack himself to put in harness. When he learns the right place for humor and learns to use his individual way of looking at things as an asset instead of a handicap, his natural gift of an individual outlook and witty expression are going to help him. . . . We must allow for a period of adjustment and growing up; and the final product is often more interesting and more effective than the boy with a more conventional mind who has been to us parents and teachers much less trouble."

Yet Roosevelt was not naive, and he was well aware of Kennedy's reputation as a businessman who would ignore the rules to make money. Thus, when Roosevelt named Kennedy to head the securities commission, the president privately joked he wanted to "set a thief to catch a thief."[14] The senior Kennedy, however, is credited with doing a good job in establishing the new agency, which was designed to eliminate illegal business practices of "thieves" in the stock market and to insure it would never completely crash as it had in 1929.

World War II

Jack returned to Harvard in the fall of 1939 with a renewed sense of purpose, earning B's in government and economic courses. He also wrote an undergraduate thesis on Great Britain's attempts during the 1930s to deal with an aggressive European dictator, Adolf Hitler, by making a series of concessions to avoid war with Nazi Germany. This so-called policy of appeasement failed, however, and when Kennedy graduated cum laude (with honor) in the spring of 1940, Europe was already engulfed in World War II.

His father, unable to attend his son's graduation, sent a cable from England (to save characters, cables have no punctuation): "Two things I always knew about you one that you are smart and two that you are a swell guy love dad."[15]

As it did for millions of Americans, the coming war would dramatically change Kennedy's life. It would also set him on the path that would lead him to the White House.

Chapter

2 JFK: Author, War Hero

While campaigning in Ashland, Wisconsin, during the 1960 presidential primary, a high school youth flippantly asked John F. Kennedy how he became a hero during World War II. "It was easy—they sank my boat,"[16] Kennedy quipped. It was not that simple, however, and his adventure after PT 109 sank became one of the pivotal experiences of his life as well as one that contributed to his early political success.

Kennedy, like millions of young Americans, fought for his country as war engulfed the world for the second time in his life. But before he became a war hero, the gangling young aristocrat wrote a best-selling book on how World War II began. The book was, of course, based on his Harvard senior thesis, a work with the unwieldy title, "Appeasement at Munich: The Inevitable Result of the Slowness of the British Democracy to Change from a Disarmament Policy."

Many historians believe that England could have prevented World War II, which was ignited by Adolf Hitler's thirst for conquest, by refusing to allow the Nazi dictator to take parts of Czechoslovakia and other territory he seized in the 1930s. Historians contend that Hitler would have backed down if England and other nations had banded together at that time in opposition. But England backed away from a

confrontation, enabling Germany to build up its military power; on September 1, 1939, Hitler's army invaded Poland, touching off World War II.

In his thesis, Kennedy argued that a democracy will always lag behind a dictatorship in preparing for war. "In a dictatorship," he pointed out, "a vigorous armaments program can be carried on, even though the people are deeply hostile to the idea of going to war."[17] Because England needed so much time to build up its military to counter Germany, Kennedy believed, Prime Minister Neville Chamberlain had no choice but to let Hitler have his way during the 1930s.

One of Kennedy's main contentions was that a totalitarian government, in which all decisions are made by one individual or a small group, can act more quickly than a democracy. While Hitler simply ordered all his nation's resources to be channeled into military spending, English leaders had to plead with voters to raise taxes to do the same thing. Their efforts at first were unsuccessful, and by the time popular opinion shifted to supporting a war effort, Hitler had become too strong to stop.

Kennedy's book became popular when it was published in 1940 because the United States was facing the same dilemma: Should it increase its military strength because of the threat of German or Japanese aggression? Kennedy said England's fate held the key to that answer:

I say therefore that we cannot afford to let England's experience pass unnoticed. Now that the world is ablaze, America has awakened to the problems facing it. But in the past, we have repeatedly refused to appropriate money for defense. We can't escape the fact that democracy in America, like democracy in England, has been asleep at the switch.[18]

Kennedy's critics later used this book to claim he disliked democracy and was a totalitarian at heart. But Kennedy was only

---

Why England Slept

In Why England Slept, *John F. Kennedy argues that dictatorships like Germany have an advantage over democracies in making decisions. This understanding would later help him cope with the threat from the Soviet Union when he was president. His belief that a democracy can meet such a challenge only if its citizens make personal sacrifices is a theme he would also raise in his inaugural speech.*

"We should recognize the advantage that a dictatorship has in preparing for modern warfare. If Britain is defeated, and we are in competition with the dictatorships [of Japan and Germany], both economically and in trying to build up armaments, we shall be at a definite disadvantage. . . . We shall have the realization to sustain us that over the long run we can outlast them; but while the menace is there, all groups must be prepared to sacrifice many of the particular group interests for the national interest. By voluntary effort, we must be prepared to equal the centralized efforts of the dictators."

Kennedy also stresses the need for America to be militarily strong before it has to resort to war. He would follow through on this as president by presiding over the largest military buildup at that time in U.S. history to meet the growing challenge from the Soviet Union:

"We must always keep our armaments equal to our commitments. . . . We must realize that any bluff will be called. We cannot tell anyone to keep out of our hemisphere unless our armaments *and the people behind these armaments* are prepared to back up the command, even to the ultimate point of going to war. There must be no doubt in anyone's mind, the decision must be automatic: if we debate, if we hesitate, if we question, it will be too late."

recognizing the very real advantage a totalitarian government has in making decisions in such a situation, and he suggested ways in which the resources of a democracy could be mobilized to stand up to a dictator's war machine. The work struck a chord with Americans, who were increasingly worried about how to respond to German and Japanese aggression around the world.

The book was strongly influenced by Kennedy's father, who was sympathetic to Chamberlain but believed Germany would triumph in any war. Although President Franklin D. Roosevelt wanted to help England, his ambassador was against U.S. intervention.

As a diplomat, Joseph P. Kennedy was a disaster. He disappointed the English by demanding U.S. neutrality and angered

Joseph P. Kennedy upon graduation from Harvard. He fulfilled his goal of becoming a millionaire by age thirty-five.

them with statements that seemed to flatter Germany. "Democracy is finished in England"[19] is one of the many comments that forced Roosevelt to seek his resignation in late 1940.

Famous Author

In 1939 Joseph Kennedy told his son he thought the Harvard thesis would make a good book—and he had powerful friends who helped get it published. *New York Times* writer Arthur Krock helped polish the manuscript and came up with a catchier title, *Why England Slept*. Henry Luce, publisher of *Time* and *Life* magazines, wrote the introduction.

Now an expanded and better-written version of the college thesis, Kennedy's book sold some eighty thousand copies, partly because his proud father bought some thirty to forty thousand copies. "You would be surprised," Kennedy told his son, "how a book that really makes the grade with high-class people stands you in good stead in years to come."[20]

The book received generally good reviews. Harold Laski, however, a professor at the London School of Economics with whom Jack briefly studied before entering Harvard, was not as lenient. After Joseph Kennedy sent him a copy, Laski responded critically:

> The easy thing for me to do would be to repeat the eulogies that Krock and Harry Luce have showered on your boy's work. In fact, I choose the more difficult way of regretting deeply that you let him publish it. For while it is the book of a lad with brains, it is very

immature, it has no structure, and dwells almost wholly on the surface of things. In a good university, half a hundred seniors do books like this as part of their normal work. I don't honestly think the publisher would have looked at that book of Jack's if he had not been your son, and if you had not been ambassador. And those are not the right grounds for publication.[21]

Kennedy Joins the Navy

After graduating from Harvard, Kennedy took some classes at Stanford University's business school. But he became bored, quit after only six months, and spent several months vacationing in Latin America. Kennedy was also suffering from ulcers, and doctors had advised him to rest and build up his health.

Although Joe Jr. had opposed U.S. participation in World War II, he enlisted in the navy in the spring of 1941. Jack, ever competitive with his brother, also decided to join the military. Despite his many medical problems, he somehow passed the navy physical and was accepted for military duty. His father arranged an appointment as an ensign in the naval reserve, and Jack was assigned to naval intelligence in Washington, D.C.

His duties were light—writing a daily news digest for the navy chief of staff—and Kennedy had plenty of time to socialize. Among the many women he dated was Inga Arvad, a beautiful Danish journalist suspected of having connections to Nazi officials in Germany. J. Edgar Hoover, who was still directing the Federal Bureau of Investigation (FBI) when Kennedy was president, secretly recorded telephone conversations between the two but was never able to prove the allegations against Arvad.

"Jack's intelligence work and Inga Arvad were incompatible," wrote Herbert S. Parmet:

[FBI files revealed] that she first came to their attention in November of 1940, when a classmate at the Columbia School of Journalism advised she may have been sent by the Germans. Her friendship with Hitler was reported by the FBI's New York office on June 7, 1941. In mid-January, the Office of Naval Intelligence informed the FBI that "Ensign Jack" had been "playing around" with her. Suddenly, Jack was reassigned to the 6th Naval District Headquarters in Charleston, South Carolina, an assignment more dignified for the Ambassador's son than discharging him from the Navy under a cloud.[22]

Kennedy Becomes a Hero

When the United States entered the war following the Japanese attack on Pearl Harbor on December 7, 1941, Jack opted for military action. He applied for a course in seamanship being offered by the navy at Northwestern University in Evanston, Illinois. It was there he fell in love with PT boats. PT stood for patrol torpedo, and duty on board the fragile plywood vessels, which were only eighty feet long, was considered daring and dangerous.

During this period Kennedy was plagued by his weak back and ulcers, which he medicated with massive quantities of ice cream, pancakes, and toasted cheese sandwiches. Partly because of his medical condition, the navy wanted Kennedy to remain stateside as an instructor. Kennedy declined, but when he learned the navy was going to assign him to Panama, he made a phone call.

"They tried to ship me to Panama," he later recalled. "So then I called the old man and told him what I wanted, that I wanted to see action. And the next day, just like that, the very next day, I had orders sending me off to this PT outfit in the Pacific."[23]

Kennedy took command of PT 109 at Tulagi, in the Solomon Islands, on April 25, 1943. There, in the South Pacific, he began fixing up the war-weary vessel and training a crew. Night patrols were dangerous for the small boats, which were easily damaged. Their strength was that they were faster and more maneuverable than larger enemy ships.

On August 1, PT 109 left on a routine mission with other PT boats to block a convoy of four Japanese destroyers—the *Amagiri, Arashi, Hagikaze,* and *Shigure*—that the navy had learned were landing men and supplies that night on the island of Munda. The convoys that moved nightly through the Blackett Strait were known as the "Japanese Express," and stopping them was a major PT boat assignment. Six destroyers and fifteen PTs went out that night to intercept the Japanese.

They failed to stop the ships. When the Japanese ships returned, the *Amagiri* came up suddenly on PT 109. Neither ship real-

How Jack Got in the Navy

Biographers differ on whether John F. Kennedy passed the navy physical as a result of a rigorous program of exercises to strengthen his back or got a free pass into the military thanks to his influential father. In A Question of Character: A Life of John F. Kennedy, *Thomas C. Reeves writes:*

"(James MacGregor) Burns and Rose Kennedy later contended that Jack tried to join the Army that spring but was rejected due to his back condition. There is no evidence of this. They also claimed that he went through five months of strengthening exercises and then passed the Navy fitness test. Careful research, however, has revealed that the ambassador pulled strings . . . to get both Joe Junior (who had a—no doubt minor—physical problem of some sort) and Jack past Navy physicians. In August a physician friend of (Capt. Alan) Kirk's gave Jack his physical. Not surprisingly, he passed. Moreover, without any training, Jack was immediately granted a commission as an ensign in the Naval Reserve. Jacks 'unstable' back should alone have disqualified him from military service. His ulcer and his asthma could have exempted him as well."

Navy lieutenant John F. Kennedy aboard PT 109 in the South Pacific in 1943. His actions after a Japanese destroyer sank his boat made him a hero and helped him win his first race for Congress three years later.

ized the other was there until the two were ready to collide. The prow of the larger Japanese destroyer sliced through the hull of Kennedy's boat and dumped most of the thirteen-man crew into the water; two men died instantly. The *Amagiri* sailed on, leaving behind the burning wreckage of PT 109 and eleven survivors floating in the Pacific.

When the fire caused by the collision finally went out, Kennedy had his crew climb aboard the bow section. The next morning, with the bow beginning to sink, Kennedy decided they should swim to Plum Pudding Island, about three-and-a-half miles away. He ordered nine of the survivors to hold on to a plank and swim while he followed, towing sailor Patrick McMahon, who had been badly burned. "Will we ever get out of this?" someone asked as they began swimming. "It can be done," Kennedy responded. "We'll do it." [24]

A strong swimmer, Kennedy towed McMahon through the water by a long strap from McMahon's life jacket that he clenched in his teeth. The swim took five hours, and by the time they crawled ashore it had been fifteen hours since the collision.

That night Kennedy swam out into Ferguson Passage, another channel, in an effort to spot a friendly ship. He was unsuccessful. The next evening another sailor made the swim but also saw no one. The next day the survivors swam to another nearby island, where they could find coconuts to eat. Kennedy and George "Barney" Ross then decided to swim to nearby Naru Island, which was closer to the sea route used by PT boats.

On Naru Island they came upon some friendly natives who were willing to carry a message to a nearby Australian coast watcher, Lieutenant Arthur Reginald Evans. Kennedy used his knife to scratch the following message on a coconut, a war souvenir that he would display years later on his White House desk:

NATIVE KNOWS POSIT
HE CAN PILOT 11 ALIVE NEED
SMALL BOAT
KENNEDY[25]

PT boats rescued the eleven men, and they returned to their base August 8. Kennedy received the Navy and Marine Corps Medal for "courage, endurance and excellent leadership" for conduct that helped save lives and was "in keeping with the highest traditions of the United States Naval Service."[26]

Kennedy took command of a new boat, PT 59, and stayed in the Pacific until December, when he was shipped home because his ailing back, ulcers, and malaria had weakened him and dropped his weight to 125 pounds.

Family Tragedy and a New Career

Kennedy, who had been a PT boat instructor in Miami, left that posting to enter Chelsea Naval Hospital near Boston for back surgery. In June 1944 he had a disc operation, the first of several he would have over the years to alleviate his back problems, but the surgery was unsuccessful.

The summer of 1944 was tragic for the Kennedy family. On August 12 the family learned that Joe Jr. had been killed when an experimental bomber he had been flying exploded during a test flight. On September 10 Billy Hartington, husband of Kathleen Kennedy, was killed while fighting in France.

In early 1945, after a long stay in the hospital, Kennedy left the service and tried his hand at journalism. He was hired as a special correspondent for International News Service, a wire service owned by the Hearst newspaper chain. Touted as "the PT hero who would explain the GI viewpoint,"[27] Kennedy wrote stories about the first United Nations meetings in San Francisco and elections in England.

The war was nearly over and Kennedy soon abandoned the idea of a career in journalism. Instead, Kennedy decided to run for a seat in Congress. His "decision" to face voters in his native Boston in 1946, however, is another of those Kennedy events shrouded in myth.

Most accounts claim that Joseph Kennedy had planned on having his eldest son

PT 109

Perhaps Lieutenant John F. Kennedy's most heroic act in the PT 109 incident was to help wounded Patrick McMahon make the initial swim from the sinking boat to Plum Pudding Island. He towed McMahon through the water for five hours. The following account is from PT 109: John F. Kennedy in World War II *by Robert J. Donovan.*

"'I'll take McMahon with me,' he [Kennedy] said. 'The rest of you can swim together on this plank.'

McMahon, sure that death was only a matter of time, remained silent when Kennedy helped him into the water, which stung his burns cruelly. In the back of his kapok [life jacket] a three-foot-long strap ran from the top to a buckle near the bottom. Kennedy swam around behind him and tried to unbuckle it, but the strap had grown so stiff from immersion that it wouldn't slide through. McMahon was surprised at the matter-of-fact way Kennedy went about it. It was as if he did this sort of thing every day. After tugging the strap a few times Kennedy took out his knife and cut it. Then he clamped the loose end in his teeth and began swimming the breast stroke. He and McMahon were back to back. Kennedy was low in the water under McMahon, who was floating along on his back with his head behind Kennedy's.

Near sundown on August 2 Kennedy and Pat McMahon half drifted up on the southeastern trim of Plum Pudding Island. Reaching the clean white sand seemed to be the ultimate limit of Kennedy's endurance. His aching jaws released the strap of McMahon's kapok, the end of which was pockmarked with Kennedy's tooth marks. . . . Swimming with the strap in his teeth Kennedy had swallowed quantities of salt water. When he stood he vomited until he fell again in exhaustion."

---

enter politics, with the goal of one day becoming president. When Joe Jr. was killed, he simply ordered John to take Joe's place. "I got Jack into politics," his father once boasted. "I was the one. I told him Joe was dead and that it was therefore his responsibility to run for office." [28] Jack Kennedy himself once admitted: "It was like being drafted. My father wanted his eldest son in politics. 'Wanted' isn't the right word. He demanded it. You know my father." [29]

Some biographers, however, have tried to deny the stories told by the Kennedys, father and son. Arthur M. Schlesinger Jr., a top aide to Kennedy when he was president, wrote: "He entered the political arena—*not*

In 1946 John F. Kennedy's father (top) and grandfather (left) helped him win his first election. Joseph P. Kennedy provided money and helped organize Jack's campaign while John F. "Honey Fitz" Fitzgerald gave his grandson a political legacy and name recognition in Boston.

to take Joe's place, as is often alleged, not to compete subconsciously with him, but as an expression of his own ideals and interests."[30]

The seat in the House of Representatives had opened when incumbent James Curley, a legendary Boston politician and old adversary of Honey Fitz, vacated it to run for mayor. It was the perfect opportu-

nity for Kennedy, who returned to Boston to capitalize on the family name.

Kennedy's motivation for entering politics is less important, however, than the result of his decision to file for candidacy in the Eleventh Congressional District of Massachusetts. A future president was about to begin his political career.

3 JFK Goes to Washington

On the night in June 1946 that John F. Kennedy won the primary race for a seat in Congress, his grandfather, the colorful old politician John F. "Honey Fitz" Fitzgerald, danced a jig on a table and sang his trademark song "Sweet Adeline."

Kennedy had convincingly beaten ten other candidates to win the Democratic nomination for the seat Honey Fitz once held, rolling up almost twice as many votes (22,183) as runner-up Michael Neville. Because Boston was a Democratic stronghold, the primary was the *real* election, and in November Kennedy overwhelmed Republican candidate Lester W. Bowen 60,093 votes to only 26,007.

The impromptu celebration by Honey Fitz was fitting because Kennedy's family played a great part in his victory. His father supplied funds, recruited Joe Kane, a veteran politician and cousin of the Kennedys, to help run the campaign, and used his connections with local and national news media to get his son favorable coverage; brother Robert was a valuable worker; his mother, Rose, and sisters Jean, Eunice, and Pat campaigned door-to-door and held house parties and formal teas; and even fourteen-year-old Teddy ran errands.

Kennedy—thin and anemic-looking, obviously weakened by his war experiences—drove himself relentlessly and built a strong personal organization. His drive and organizational skills would become hallmarks of all his campaigns.

Kennedy Power

The Eleventh Congressional District was a working-class area whose residents revered the Kennedys as an immigrant family that had made good. The candidate moved into a small apartment at 122 Bowdoin Street, which became his voting address for the rest of his life.

The Kennedy drawing power was shown by a formal tea at the Commander Hotel in Cambridge. Hundreds of women formed a line that extended from the lobby of the hotel, across the street, and into a nearby park. They seemed more interested in the Kennedy women and what they wore than the candidate. "For all of them," Rose Kennedy remembered, "there were handshakes and smiles from each of us. There were a few men there, but most were women, all of whom seemed to have had their hair done for the event. Jack was marvelous with them."[31]

Kennedy won voters with the force of his personality and natural charm. He used those same qualities to woo campaign workers like Dave Powers, an ex-serviceman who joined Kennedy's campaign after listening to him address a group of Gold Star Mothers, women who had lost a son in the war. Kennedy talked of the wartime sacrifices people made, the need for lasting peace, and the responsibilities of the veterans who survived. He ended by saying, "I think I know how all you mothers feel. You see, my mother is a Gold Star mother, too." The women surrounded him lovingly, saying how much he reminded them of their own sons. Powers, who would remain at Kennedy's side through his presidency, was impressed. "You were terrific. I've never seen such a reaction," he said. When Kennedy asked him if he would work for him, Powers said, "I've already started working for you."[32]

It was Kennedy's ability to touch the hearts of people from all walks of life that enabled a millionaire's son who had not lived in Boston for many years to win votes in that first election and many others; in fact, he never lost an election. "He could talk with humble people and understand them as if he had been with them all his life. He could walk in and get along with them and understand them as well as if he had been brought up among them,"[33] said Edward McLaughlin, who met Kennedy in the Pacific and later headed the Boston City Council.

However, the small talk of politics did not come easily at first for Kennedy. Thomas P. "Tip" O'Neill, a Boston congressman who later became Speaker of the House, remembers: "He hated crowds [when he began campaigning]. When we went into a hall together, he'd immediately look for the back door. It was said that Jack Kennedy was the only [politician] in Boston who never went to a wake unless he had known the deceased personally."[34] But Kennedy gave more than 450 speeches in his first campaign and forced himself to learn how to walk up to strangers on the street or in a bar and chat with them as if they were old friends.

The Kennedy campaign slogan was "The New Generation Offers a Leader," and he ran on bread-and-butter economic issues—jobs, affordable housing, medical care, veterans benefits, and broadening Social Security. His stands were not much different than those of his opponents.

But he had the Kennedy name and connections and his status as a war hero. In 1944 respected author John Hersey had written about Kennedy's PT 109 heroics in the *New Yorker* magazine. Joe Kennedy used his influence to have the article reprinted in *Reader's Digest,* which had a far greater circulation. During the campaign tens of thousands of copies of Hersey's piece were distributed throughout the district. Kennedy later regretted having leaned on his war experiences so heavily: "There's something wrong about parlaying a sunken PT boat into a congressional seat."[35]

However, Kennedy was no more guilty than scores of other veterans who capitalized on the war. One of the former servicemen also elected to Congress in 1946 was Richard M. Nixon of California, whom Kennedy would face fourteen years later in the 1960 presidential election.

Representative Kennedy

Kennedy was twenty-nine when he took his seat in January 1947, but he looked much younger. That, coupled with his penchant for casual dress—he often wore khaki pants, a wrinkled seersucker jacket, and a food-spotted tie—resulted in his being mistaken for a House page. "Well, how do you like that?" he demanded in mock indignation as he burst into his office one morning. "Some people got into the elevator and asked me for the fourth floor!"[36]

The first big issue Kennedy tackled was low-cost housing. Few homes or apartments had been built since 1929: First the Great Depression had dried up funds, and then World War II had consumed all available resources and labor. Millions of people, many of them former servicemen who returned home to marry and start raising families, were living with relatives, in garages, basements, and anywhere else they could find space.

Kennedy, who shared a comfortable townhouse in Georgetown with his sister Eunice, was committed to helping others

First Campaign

In One Brief Shining Moment: Remembering Kennedy, *biographer William Manchester, who knew the candidate at the time, writes that John F. Kennedy drove himself to exhaustion in his first campaign.*

"By 6:00 A.M. each day he was standing beside cold, dark factory gates, or waterfront docks, or the Charlestown Navy Yard, shaking hands with arriving workmen. At 8:15, when the last of them had punched his time card, he would have breakfast in a diner. At nine o'clock he was back on the job, making calls in the tenements like a door-to-door salesman, astounding and then delighting housewives. Afternoons would be spent strolling streets, shaking hands on corners, meat markets, taverns, department stores, fire stations, police stations, and barbershops. Evening would be spent in a whirlwind tour of at least a half-dozen house parties, the typical volunteer hostess being a typist, switchboard operator, or schoolteacher who would gaze at him with star struck eyes while he sipped cokes and nibbled sandwiches, stealing furtive glances at his watch. . . .

It was said the night before the election he and several friends were driving down a street when he saw an old woman trying to cross the street. 'Stop!' ordered the candidate. He leaped out and helped the woman hobble over to the opposite curb. When he returned somebody in the back seat blurted out: 'You really do want them all, don't you.'"

Jack Kennedy campaigns in Boston in 1946. Like many other veterans of World War II, Kennedy capitalized on his combat record to win votes. But his celebrity as a war hero was only one of the factors that helped him win his first election.

obtain decent housing. He sponsored a housing bill to aid veterans and low-income workers, but it was opposed by many groups, including the powerful American Legion, an organization for former members of the nation's armed forces.

The legion sided with the real estate industry, which opposed government involvement in housing. The measure failed. The next year Kennedy introduced another bill to provide federal funds to eradicate slums and provide low-rent public housing. Again the powerful American Legion fought it.

This time the Massachusetts Democrat reacted angrily on the House floor: "The leadership of the American Legion has not

had a constructive thought for the benefit of the country since 1918 [the year it was founded]." [37] Taking on the revered patriotic organization was a bold move, but by late 1948 Kennedy and other Democrats finally pushed through a bill to provide government financing for veterans housing.

The incident showed the maverick style that made Congressman Kennedy hard to categorize as either conservative or liberal. It also showed that Kennedy, unlike many elected officials, was willing to stand up for what he thought was right.

On foreign affairs Kennedy at first adopted the views of his conservative father. "I'd just come out of my father's house and those were the things I knew." [38]

Thus, when communists won control of China in 1948, Kennedy harshly criticized the administration of President Harry Truman for "having lost" China. "The responsibility for the failure of our foreign policy in the Far East rests squarely with the White House and the Department of State. The House must now assume the responsibility of preventing the onrushing tide of Communism from engulfing all of Asia,"[39] Kennedy said.

Kennedy also opposed foreign aid and seemed to be an isolationist like his father. However, his views shifted as he gradually pulled away from his father's influence.

The gap between father and son emerged clearly in 1951. In December 1950 Joseph Kennedy urged the United States to get out of Korea, a country it would defend against communism in the Korean War, which began that June. He also said the United States should quit trying to protect Europe against the Soviet Union because that role was not in the country's best interests.

After a fact-finding trip to Europe, Jack told a Senate committee in February 1951 that the United States needed to keep Europe free. When asked if he was disagreeing with his father, Kennedy said, "To him and to a lot of other Americans, it looks like almost a hopeless job and that we are committing troops to be lost." Kennedy stressed it was a commitment the United States had to fulfill. "That is my position," he said. "I think you should ask my father directly as to his position."[40]

Kennedy was a liberal on the economic issues that were important to his working-class constituency: He supported social welfare programs, progressive taxation, a higher minimum wage, aid to parochial schools,

The Kennedy clan always wanted to win, whether the contest was in athletics or politics, and the entire Kennedy family helped Jack win reelection in 1948. Posing in front of the family's summer home that year in Hyannis Port, Massachusetts are (left to right) Jack, Jean, Rose, Joseph, Patricia, Robert, and Eunice. Edward, called Ted, is kneeling, holding a football.

and more government control over business, and he opposed legislation to more strictly regulate labor unions. But he favored holding the line on government spending, even if it meant less money for some social welfare programs, and he opposed a large veterans pension bill.

Biographer James MacGregor Burns explains this nearly schizophrenic voting record: "The only pattern that fits Kennedy is, on the face of it, quite simple: he was very much a representative of his Boston constituency." And the majority of his district was made up of families who were "immigrant Catholic, liberal on economic and social matters, conservative on issues of public education and civil liberties, rigidly anti-Communist, somewhat isolationist."[41]

Kennedy also never felt he had to follow the party line. "It was never drilled into me that I was responsible to some political boss in the Eleventh District,"[42] he said.

Jack Says "No!" to Curley

John Kennedy also showed his independence from conventional party politics in his first year in office. Boston mayor Jim Curley, the venerable but corrupt politician whose seat Kennedy had won, was facing imprisonment on charges of mail fraud. In an attempt to stay out of jail, Curley asked members of the Massachusetts congressional delegation to sign a plea to President Harry Truman for a pardon. Biographer James MacGregor Burns explains Kennedy's reaction in his book John Kennedy.

"It was Jim Curley who put Kennedy's independence from the Boston party and his courage to the acid test. [Representative John] McCormack drew up a petition to the President and got the prompt signatures of Massachusetts representatives, Republican and Democratic alike. Spotting Kennedy on the floor of the House, McCormack handed him the petition. Would he sign? The two men eyed each other tensely.

'Has anyone talked with the President or anything?' Kennedy asked.

'No,' said McCormack. 'If you don't want to sign it, don't sign it.'

'Well, I'm not going to sign it,' Kennedy said, and he did not. His decision was taken against the advice of close friends. McCormack was annoyed, and Curley was to seek political retribution the first chance he had. Kennedy's rebuff of Curley, long a foe of the family, took considerable courage, for the Mayor had a fanatically devoted following in Boston, especially in his old congressional district. It also reflected Kennedy's distaste for the Curley element in the party."

Playboy Image

Kennedy easily won reelection in 1948 and 1950, despite a less-than-stellar reputation as a legislator.

Victor Lasky, who wrote the first book critical of Kennedy in 1963, comments on the politician's early career:

> As even his most ardent admirers have conceded, John F. Kennedy's six years as a member of the House of Representatives were hardly marked by initiative, diligence, or courage. Kennedy himself has acknowledged that his record as a Congressman was not the most distinguished. . . . "After all," he [once said], "I wasn't equipped for the job. I didn't plan to get into it, and when I started out as a Congressman, there were lots of things I didn't know, a lot of mistakes I made, maybe some votes that should have been different."[43]

Kennedy was accused by some of spending more time chasing women than doing his job. As biographer Herbert S. Parmet writes, "Finding women and having a good time was never hard for Jack Kennedy. He had charm, intelligence, and, of greater importance, money and power. He dated all kinds of women; it didn't seem to matter, as long as they were attractive. Most were dates that he would take to a movie, his favorite diversion next to football."[44]

He also swam, sailed, played touch football and even spent time at high school football practices, as in this incident from the book *Triumph and Tragedy: The Story of the Kennedys:*

> Watching a high school practice, he asked to borrow a uniform and joined the workout. "Hey kid," a halfback yelled at him, "come on over here and snag some passes." Kennedy did. A few minutes later the coach asked the high school halfback: "How's the Congressman doing?" "Is that what they call him?" the halfback asked. "He needs a lot of work, coach. What year's he in [in high school]?"[45]

Kennedy's Health

Kennedy's health continued to trouble him. In addition to his bad back, allergies, stomach problems, and bouts with malaria, Kennedy had developed symptoms of Addison's disease, a life-threatening illness.

In the summer of 1947, Kennedy had gone to Europe to study overseas labor problems. He ended that trip by visiting his sister Kathleen in England. Kennedy became ill in London and was hospitalized before being shipped home aboard the *Queen Mary.* He arrived in New York so near death that he was given the last rites of his church before being flown to a hospital in Boston, where physicians confirmed the diagnosis of Addison's disease, which weakens the immune system and makes a person more susceptible to infectious illness.

The doctor in England had told those in Kennedy's party, "That young American friend of yours, he hasn't got a year to live."[46] His pessimism was based on what he believed to be the lack of adequate treatment for the disease. But Kennedy began receiving daily injections of DOCA (desoxycorticosterone acetate) and later had DOCA pellets implanted in his thighs to release the medication gradually into his system.

Covering Up Addison's

When John F. Kennedy was diagnosed with Addison's disease in 1947, he kept it from the news media, fearing knowledge of the illness would hurt his political career. It was a lie that would live until after he was elected president. His office said the illness was an attack of malaria from his service in the Pacific. In Jack: The Struggles of John F. Kennedy, *Herbert S. Parmet recounts the cover-up.*

"On October 25 the *Boston Post* reported that the congressman had 'been ill for the past seven weeks with malaria' and had been released by the Lahey clinic. From there he had gone to Hyannis Port for a two-week recuperation before returning to Boston. By early December political writer Bill Mullins was telling readers that Kennedy was back on the job, 'entirely recovered from the attack of Navy-born malaria which laid him low in England several months ago.' Obviously, the press merely reported family handouts."

Parmet said the lie was abetted by some Kennedy biographers including Arthur M. Schlesinger Jr. in A Thousand Days: John F. Kennedy in the White House.

"Although the book was published after [Kennedy's] death, readers were told that Jack Kennedy did not have Addison's in the classic sense—that is, caused by tuberculosis of the adrenal glands—that he had not had tuberculosis in any form and that, with modern methods of treatments, his adrenal insufficiency—evidently induced by the long night of swimming during the PT 109 episode, and the subsequent malaria—presented no serious problem."

In 1949 Kennedy began taking daily oral doses of cortisone, a newly developed steroid hormone that enabled him to live a fairly normal life; however, the illness continued to take its toll on him. In 1951, while on a trip to Japan, he became seriously ill, running a temperature of 106 degrees and once again nearly dying.

Following the family tradition of covering up unpleasant aspects of their lives, Kennedy hid the condition, ordering his staff in 1947 to say he had suffered another attack of malaria. It was a lie he would repeat for many years. In fact, the day after he won the 1960 presidential election he stated: "I never had Addison's disease. In regard to my health, it was fully explained in a press statement in the middle of July, and my health is excellent."[47]

4 Senator Kennedy: Success, Love, Pain

It did not take John F. Kennedy long to realize that being one of more than 430 representatives did not suit his personality. "For one thing," he said, "we were just worms in the House—nobody pays much attention to us nationally."[48] The anonymity and lack of status were galling to someone who needed center stage.

Another factor in deciding to seek higher office was his own sense of mortality, honed by his many near-fatal illnesses and the deaths of his brother Joe and his favorite sister, Kathleen, who was killed in a 1949 plane crash. "The point is," he once said, "that you've got to live every day like it's your last day on earth. That's what I'm doing."[49]

After winning reelection in 1950 by an almost 5 to 1 margin, Kennedy decided to move up from the House of Representatives by challenging Republican Henry Cabot Lodge Jr., who had been a senator since 1936. The 1952 election would include a bit of family revenge: Lodge's grandfather had beaten Kennedy's grandfather in the 1916 Senate race.

Kennedy again drove himself at a fierce pace, visiting all 39 cities and 312 towns in Massachusetts before the election and then enduring a whirlwind schedule in 1952. Kennedy again built a strong grassroots organization, with 286 local secretaries and 20,000 volunteers.

His family again rallied around him and twenty-six-year-old Robert, who was fresh out of the University of Virginia's law school, ran his campaign. Robert gave one of the shortest political speeches in history when no other Kennedy was available: "My brother Jack couldn't be here. My mother couldn't be here. My sister Eunice couldn't be here. My sister Pat couldn't be here. My sister Jean couldn't be here. But if my brother Jack were here, he'd tell you Lodge has a very bad voting record. Thank you."[50]

Kennedy's sisters and mother once again held teas and house parties. Biographer James MacGregor Burns describes an elegant tea at the Commander Hotel in Cambridge:

> The star of the affair was Rose Kennedy. Still youthful-looking and stylish in a dignified way, she gave a simple motherly tribute to her son that made the real campaign seem far off and somehow unimportant. Sisters Eunice, Jean, and Pat managed the affairs with their usual charm and gusto. The candidate gave a short talk, barely touching on issues and ending with a request that each of the ladies come up on the stage so that he and his mother and sisters could meet them and later have a cup of tea with them.[51]

A Grueling Senate Race

John F. Kennedy set a punishing pace for himself in the 1952 Senate race. Kennedy biographer Herbert S. Parmet in Jack: The Struggles of John F. Kennedy *describes how it took its toll on the candidate.*

"On the road he seldom got a full night's sleep, often depending on the rest he could get from throwing his head back on a backseat pillow [in a car going from event to event], while subsisting on cheeseburgers and malteds. At a Springfield fire station he succumbed to the impulse to demonstrate his agility by sliding down a fire pole from the third floor to the first. When he hit bottom, he doubled up with pain. The reaggravation of his back made crutches indispensable. But still he tried to keep his agony private, while the managers [of his campaign] feared the potency of Kennedy's physical condition as a campaign issue. [People] were informed he had 'suffered a recurrence of an old war injury to his back a few weeks ago,' a not-so-subtle re-evocation of sympathy for the war hero. Before entering a hall for a speech, [Dave] Powers would take his crutches and place them outside the auditorium, unseen by the crowd. He often stood for several hours on receiving lines while in severe pain."

An estimated 65,000 to 70,000 people, mostly women, attended 23 such events.

The Kennedys came up with a technological innovation on campaigning—two televised campaign promotions called "Coffee with the Kennedys." While family members chatted on television, campaign workers hosted parties in their homes.

Running things in the background was Joseph Kennedy, who once said: "It takes three things to win in politics. The first is money, the second is money, and the third is money."[52] He provided this essential commodity—some accounts say several million dollars, even though official campaign reports only listed $349,646—and used his influence in many other ways.

A minor scandal surfaced several years later when it was revealed that during the Senate campaign, the senior Kennedy had made a $500,000 loan to John Fox, owner of the *Boston Post* newspaper. Kennedy insisted that the loan was a simple business deal but the newspaper, normally Republican, supported Kennedy.

When the votes were counted, Kennedy was the winner by more than 70,000 ballots: 1,211,984 to 1,141,247. Lodge never knew what hit him. The Kennedy victory was especially surprising because Republican Dwight D. Eisenhower had won Massachusetts by more than 200,000 votes that year in his successful race for the presidency.

As Burns comments, "The campaign was not won on issues; the differences between the men were too obscure. Like most congressional and many senatorial campaigns, the outcome turned on personality rather than national policies."[53]

A defeated Lodge complained: "It was those damn tea parties that beat me."[54]

Jack and Jackie

On January 3, 1953, John F. Kennedy was sworn in as a U.S. senator. It was also the year he married Jacqueline Lee Bouvier, who would become one of the most popular first ladies in history.

Kennedy met Bouvier in 1951 at a dinner party in Georgetown hosted by mutual friend Charles Bartlett. Kennedy was already campaigning for the Senate and Bouvier was a senior at George Washington University. "I leaned across the asparagus and asked for a date,"[55] Kennedy said. His future wife turned him down, but they began a long-distance romance.

Bouvier describes their early relationship:

It was a very spasmodic courtship. We didn't see each other for six months, because I went to Europe again and Jack began his summer and fall campaigning in Massachusetts. Then came six months when we were both back. Jack was in Congress and I was in my

Kennedy's mother and sisters appeared on two "Coffee with the Kennedys" telecasts to win voters in his 1952 Senate race. Pat is seated to the left of her mother, Jean stands next to the candidate, and Eunice models a poodle skirt, popular in this period, that is decorated with his name and the Democratic donkey.

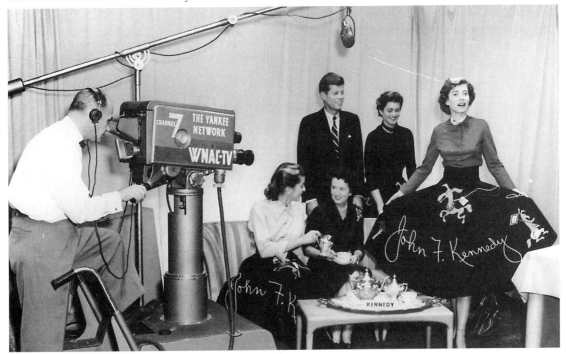

last year of [college]. But it was still spasmodic because he spent half of each week in Massachusetts. He'd call me from some oyster bar up there, with a great clinking of coins, to ask me out to the movies the following Wednesday in Washington.[56]

Like Kennedy, Bouvier grew up in luxury. She was the daughter of John Vernon "Black Jack" Bouvier III and Janet Lee. The couple divorced when she was seventeen, and in 1942 her mother married Hugh D. Auchincloss, a twice-divorced millionaire. Bouvier and her sister, Lee, lived with their mother and Auchincloss.

Jackie studied at Vassar and at the Sorbonne in France before attending a third prestigious college, George Washington University. Upon graduation in 1951 she took a job with the *Washington Times-Herald* as the "Inquiring Camera Girl." For $42.50

a week she photographed and interviewed prominent people. On April 21, 1953, her column included a picture of Kennedy and his whimsical observation: "I've often thought that the country might be better off if we Senators and Pages traded jobs."[57]

Their romance picked up after Kennedy won his Senate seat, and he escorted her to President Eisenhower's inaugural ball. They were married September 12, 1953, in St. Mary's Roman Catholic Church in Newport, Rhode Island.

The Senator

As a senator, Kennedy began to specialize in education, labor, and foreign policy issues, becoming a more active legislator and taking his duties more seriously.

Taking Care of Constituents

In John Kennedy, *James MacGregor Burns writes that when Kennedy became a senator he concentrated on helping his constituents.*

"The Senator's office soon gained a reputation for prompt action on constituents' requests. And as the reputation grew, so did the volume of favors sought. Some were routine: requests for copies of government documents, for help on application for veterans benefits, for information on passports and the like. Some were more troublesome: a professor's request for study space in the Library of Congress, a small businessman needing guidance through Washington's bureaucratic maze, a disappointed father anxious to know why his son was turned down at Harvard or Georgetown. Could the Senator do anything about it? In an amazing number of cases, the Senator [meaning his staff] usually did."

John F. Kennedy and Jacqueline Lee Bouvier joyously cut their wedding cake after being married September 12, 1953, the year Kennedy took office as a senator. Their marriage, however, would be marred by his marital infidelities.

In 1953 he hired twenty-four-year-old Theodore Sorensen as a speechwriter. An attorney who had worked for a Senate subcommittee, Sorensen was an unabashed liberal, and many biographers feel Sorensen influenced Kennedy's political move toward liberalism. Sorensen claims Kennedy came into his own as a lawmaker in his second year in the Senate:

Some might say that he fiddled around as a Congressman and really didn't become interested until his sophomore year in the Senate. It seemed to me in 1953 that an inner struggle was being waged for the spirit of John Kennedy—

a struggle between the political dilettante and the statesman, between the lure of luxury and lawmaking.[58]

Kennedy was ready to take a stand that was unpopular back home, and in 1954 he went against state interests by supporting the St. Lawrence Seaway. The seaway would be good for the national economy by opening the Great Lakes to international shipping, but Massachusetts congressmen had routinely voted against it because it could hurt the port of Boston. "I am unable to accept such a narrow view of my function as United States Senator,"[59] he said.

He became the first member of Congress from New England to appoint an African American to his staff. Kennedy also supported abolition of the poll tax, a tactic southern states used to keep African Americans from voting; sponsored anti-lynching legislation; and tried to amend Senate rules on filibusters, which southerners used to kill legislation that would give African Americans more rights.

The issue that won Kennedy the most attention was his pursuit of corrupt union officials, part of his duties as chairman of the Senate Labor Subcommittee, which investigated criminal allegations against labor leaders. Kennedy's group became known as the Labor Rackets Committee, and his brother Robert was its legal counsel. The hearings were televised, and the dramatic confrontations between the Kennedys and labor leaders helped introduce the brothers to the public. Subcommittee findings resulted in jail sentences for union leaders on various charges, including mishandling union dues.

But on other labor issues, Kennedy remained true to his party's pro-union stance. For example, he favored a so-called bill of rights for labor in 1959 and managed to soften measures labor opposed in the Senate version, which passed by a vote of 90 to 1.

In January 1957 Kennedy won a coveted assignment to the Foreign Relations Committee. This was one of his main areas of interest, and he began writing articles for publications like the scholarly journal *Foreign Affairs*. In one piece he attacked the Eisenhower administration's foreign policy for failing to consider "new realities" such as the rising tide of nationalism around the world and the effects of the breakup of European colonies in Africa and Southeast Asia. "Many of the old conceptions of war and peace, friend and foe, victory and defeat," Kennedy wrote, "must be reshaped in the light of new realities."[60]

Kennedy was instrumental in defeating a 1956 effort to change the way presidential elections are decided. The president and vice president are not elected by popular vote but by electoral votes they receive by winning a majority of votes in individual states. Representatives of individual states then cast those votes in the electoral college in Washington, D.C., after the election.

Southern senators had wanted to allow the electoral votes of the individual states to be divided between candidates instead of being cast as one unit. Kennedy helped kill the measure because he felt it violated the intent of Article XII of the Constitution.

Another Operation, Another Best-Seller

Ever since his unsuccessful surgery in 1944, Kennedy's back condition had been getting worse. By late May 1954 Kennedy was in severe pain, using crutches almost constantly to walk, and his weight had dropped from a healthy 180 to 140 pounds.

That summer Kennedy decided on another operation: "I'd rather be dead than spend the rest of my life on these things [crutches],"[61] he said. Because Addison's disease weakened his immune system, that feisty declaration almost came true.

On October 21, at the New York Hospital for Special Surgery, doctors fused two of his vertebrae. The operation was termed a success, but three days later Kennedy developed a urinary tract infection, became

Their Marriage

Kennedy critic Thomas C. Reeves, in A Question of Character: A Life of John F. Kennedy, *explains how Jack and Jackie Kennedy tried to shape their public image through the media.*

"Edward R. Murrow's popular CBS television program Person to Person visited [the Kennedys] a month after their [wedding]. Jackie seemed a bit nervous and Jack's responses were obviously prepared in advance, but both came across as attractive, sincere, and devoted to one another. In feature stories in several newspaper they were made to appear 'as a modest, hardworking, and romantic collegiate couple.'"

Author Reeves says both Jack and Jackie were fine actors who, throughout their marriage, were able to hide their marital problems from the news media and the public. Reeves said the marriage was difficult for Jackie for several reasons, from the Kennedy family itself to her husband's unfaithfulness.

"Jackie's introduction to Jack's siblings at Hyannis Port left her exhausted and irritated. She disliked the boisterous teasing about her name (the girls joked that she pronounced her name 'Jacklean' to rhyme with 'queen'), her clothing, and her large (size ten) feet. She was also turned off by the intense athletic competition. She tried at first to participate in the roughhouse games but quickly realized she could not take the physical punishment. 'They'll kill me before I ever get to marry him,' she told her sister. 'I swear they will.' She later broke an ankle playing touch football with Teddy. Jackie termed the Kennedy women 'the rah-rah girls.' They in turn referred to her as 'the debutante,' and made fun of what they called her 'babykins voice.'. . .

The most difficult problem Jackie faced was her husband's flagrant philandering. She had not expected total devotion . . . but she had not dreamed of the extent to which Jack would pursue other women. . . .

[Nonetheless,] a sort of friendship grew between the two. They learned to enjoy each other's company. Jackie took delight in surprising Jack with small gifts. Jack, when he paid attention, found his wife consistently interesting."

A rare picture of John F. Kennedy using crutches during his 1952 Senate campaign. Although Kennedy needed crutches at times to ease his constant back pain, he tried not to be seen using them in public. His mother is visible behind him.

seriously ill, and slipped into a coma. Although again given the last rites of his church, Kennedy rallied. But his recovery took months, and after several weeks he was taken to his family's winter home in Palm Beach.

In February 1955 Kennedy returned to New York for a second operation to remove a silver plate that was inserted during the first operation and to have a bone graft; the plate had caused another infection, and his back had not healed. He became seriously ill again and nearly died.

Following the surgery, aide Dave Powers, who was by then a close person-

al friend, watched the dressing being changed. He noted that Kennedy "had a hole in his back big enough for me to put my fist into it up to the wrist."[62] This time Kennedy's back healed, and he returned to the Senate May 23.

Kennedy had been in severe pain during both periods of convalescence. "Jack couldn't sleep for more than an hour or so at a time because his pain was so bad," his father said. "So he'd study to get his mind off the pain. That's where the book came from."[63]

The book *Profiles in Courage* is a study of famous men who had shown personal and moral courage on controversial issues. While recuperating, Kennedy read about how John Quincy Adams, Daniel Webster, George Norris, Robert A. Taft, and others had displayed the trait he so admired, and he decided to write a book on these political figures. It was published in 1956, and the next year it won the Pulitzer Prize for biography.

Some people, however, claimed that his speechwriter, Theodore Sorensen, was the main author. On December 7, 1957, television commentator Drew Pearson charged that Kennedy's book had been "ghostwritten." Pearson retracted the statement after Kennedy threatened legal action.

In the biography *Kennedy,* Sorensen flatly denies the charge: "The work was a tonic to his spirits and a distraction from his pain. And of all the abuse he would receive throughout his life, none would make him more angry than the charge a few months later that he had not written his own book."[64] Sorensen admitted he and other aides helped the bedridden Kennedy with research but that the senator wrote the book.

Sorensen's final revenge was to write the statement Pearson read on television: "I was not the author of Jack Kennedy's book—but I had 'ghost-written' ABC's statement of retraction and regret."[65]

Kennedy biographer Herbert S. Parmet, however, claims "the senator served principally as an overseer or, more charitably, as a sponsor and editor, one whose final approval was as important for its publication as for its birth. . . . The burdens of time and literary craftsmanship were clearly Sorensen's."[66]

The McCarthy Affair

Ironically, at the same time that Kennedy was working on *Profiles in Courage,* he was being criticized for failing to show political courage of his own by standing up to Senator Joe McCarthy. The Wisconsin Republican became infamous for his tactics of using unsubstantiated accusations in an attempt to unmask people in government, the arts, and entertainment whom he suspected of being communists. On December 2, 1954,

---

Profiles in Courage

In Profiles in Courage, *John F. Kennedy discusses the nature of courage in political life.*

"In no other occupation but politics is it expected that a man will sacrifice honors . . . and his chosen career on a single issue. Lawyers, businessmen, teachers, doctors, all face difficult personal decisions involving their integrity—but few, if any, face them in the glare of the spotlight as do those in public office. [For a U.S. senator] when that roll is called he cannot hide, he cannot equivocate, he cannot delay—and he senses that his constituency, like the Raven in Poe's poem, is perched there on his Senate desk, croaking 'Nevermore' as he casts the vote that stakes his political future. . . .

In whatever arena of life one may meet the challenge of courage, whatever may be the sacrifices he faces if he follows his conscience—the loss of his friends, his fortune, his contentment, even the esteem of his fellow men—each man must decide for himself the course he will follow. The stories of past courage can define that ingredient—they can teach, they can offer hope, they can provide inspiration. But they cannot supply courage itself. For this each man must look into his own soul."

---

the Senate voted 67 to 22 to censure Mc-Carthy because of his many unfounded allegations, wild statements, and increasingly bizarre behavior.

The breaking point for senators was his criticism of a Senate committee chaired by Senator Arthur Watkins of Utah. McCarthy accused the committee of being an "involuntary agent" of the Communist Party and declared that the party had "now extended its tentacles to the United States Senate."[67]

Kennedy, who was hospitalized when the vote was taken, was criticized for not having his vote recorded, a courtesy extended to senators when they have a legitimate reason for being absent. Sorensen took the blame for the failure but many believed Kennedy simply did not want to cast a vote.

Senator Joseph McCarthy holds a subpoena during a session of his Senate Investigating Committee. The Wisconsin Republican was criticized for making unfounded allegations about people he claimed were communists.

Although he disliked his tactics, the excesses of McCarthy were a sensitive issue for Kennedy. The senator was an old family friend who had employed his brother Robert as an investigator, and he was a hero to Kennedy's constituents in Massachusetts. By 1954, however, the tide had turned against McCarthy, and it had seemed the opportune time for Kennedy to take a stand. His failure, however, to act had no real impact on his political career.

The 1956 Democratic Convention

When Kennedy returned to the Senate, he discovered his widely publicized illness and book had given him a much higher national profile. Magazines solicited articles from him, and he and his staff wrote pieces that further gilded his literary image. The news media began to consider him an up-and-coming Democratic star, and in 1956 he was mentioned as a possible vice presidential nominee. In such ways are political stars created.

The biggest obstacle to national office was his religion, namely the question of whether a Roman Catholic could be relied on to take actions and institute policies that might conflict with positions held by the pope and other church leaders. Many Americans automatically opposed any candidate who might be subject to such influences.

To counter those concerns, the Kennedy staff researched the issue and supplied pro-Catholic data to well-known author Fletcher Knebel, who wrote an article for *Look* magazine entitled "Can a Catholic

Kennedy Glad He Lost

Although his loss of the vice presidential nomination in 1956 would be his only political defeat, Kennedy realized it was probably the best thing that could have happened. His father had not wanted him to get the nomination because he was sure the Republicans would win again, which they did. This is how Triumph and Tragedy, *edited by Sidney C. Moody Jr., records Kennedy's reaction.*

"Joe Kennedy helped his son analyze what had happened. He told Jack that 'God was still with him, that he could be president if he wanted to be and worked hard.'

Later Jack measured the good fortune in his defeat; 'Joe [Jr.] was the star of our family. He did everything better than the rest of us. If he had lived he would have gone on in politics and he would have been elected to the House and to the Senate, as I was. And, like me, he would have gone for the vice-presidential nomination at the 1956 convention. But, unlike me, he wouldn't have been beaten. And then he and Stevenson would have been beaten by Eisenhower, and today Joe's political career would be in shambles, and he would be trying to pick up the pieces.'"

Become Vice President?" Kennedy supporters also distributed a document that claimed a Catholic would be an asset to the ticket because key northeastern states had many Catholic voters.

Kennedy went to the 1956 convention unsure if he even wanted the position. Adlai Stevenson, who lost to Dwight D. Eisenhower in 1952, was nominated again but then did a curious thing—he allowed delegates to pick his running mate instead of naming his own candidate. That set off a political melee as candidates jockeyed for votes.

After a frantic night and day of vote-seeking, Kennedy finished second on the first ballot, trailing Tennessee senator Estes Kefauver 304 votes to 483½ (half votes were allowed). Kefauver went on to win the nomination.

It was Kennedy's first taste of presidential politics, and he had loved it.

"With only four hours of work and a handful of supporters, I came [close to] winning the [vice presidential] nomination. If I work hard for four years, I ought to be able to pick up all the marbles [and the presidential nomination],"[68] he said.

5 JFK: The New Frontier

At the end of the 1958 Senate session, *New York Times* columnist James Reston wrote: "Senator Kennedy is on the make; he makes no pretense about it, and he dismisses out of hand suggestions that he is young enough to wait for some other presidential campaign. He is swinging for the fences."[69]

After the 1956 convention John F. Kennedy had set his sights on capturing the White House. Kennedy announced his candidacy January 20 in the Senate Caucus Room.

"The Presidency," he said, "is the most powerful office in the Free World. Through its leadership can come a more vital life for our people. In it are centered the hopes of the globe around us for freedom and a more secure life."[70]

Kennedy said the campaign issues were the nuclear arms race with the Soviet Union, the worldwide threat communism posed to democracy, and how to continue America's economic growth so it would benefit all citizens.

Kennedy had been campaigning informally for the presidency since the 1956 convention. That fall he worked tirelessly for the Democratic ticket, emerging from the election with his political star shining more brightly than ever. Kennedy began speaking at political events across the country, giving at least 150 speeches in 1957 and some 200 in 1958 as he accumulated political IOUs from faithful party members in every state. With the help of his staff, he continued producing magazine articles, bolstering his image as an expert on many subjects, and his father's media connections helped him gain favorable coverage so more people would learn about the young senator from Massachusetts.

By 1960 his hard work had made him the front-runner for the nomination. "In every campaign I've ever been in, they've said I was starting too early, that I would peak too soon or get too much exposure or run out of gas or be too easy a target," Kennedy said. "I would never have won any race following that advice."[71]

The Primaries

In 1960 there were two ways to get the nomination—by winning primary elections or by working behind the scenes to line up delegates for the July Democratic convention in Los Angeles. Kennedy realized he had to go the primary route to show he could win votes despite two huge handicaps—his youth and his religion.

Why He Ran at Age Forty-Three

John F. Kennedy could have waited until he was older to run for president, and many felt that he should have. In President Kennedy, *biographer Richard Reeves explains why Kennedy chose to seek the nation's highest office in 1960.*

"Looking back, it seemed to me that the most important thing about Kennedy was not a great political decision, though he made some, but his own political ambition. He did not wait his turn. He directly challenged the institution he wanted to control, the political system. . . . He believed (and proved) that the only qualification for the most powerful job in the world was wanting it. His power did not come from the top down or from the bottom up. It was an ax driven by his own ambition into the middle of the system, biting to the center he wanted for himself. When he was asked early in 1960 why he thought he should be president, he answered: 'I look around me at the others in the race, and I say to myself, 'Well, if they think they can do it why not me? Why not me? That's the answer. And I think it's enough.'"

President Kennedy seated in a rocking chair in the White House Oval Office. The motion of a rocker helped to ease his back pain.

His main competitors were Senators Lyndon B. Johnson of Texas, Stuart Symington of Missouri, and Hubert H. Humphrey of Minnesota, and two-time nominee Adlai Stevenson, a former governor of Illinois.

Only Humphrey posed a major challenge in the primaries, and their first important clash came in Wisconsin, where Humphrey had an edge because he was from neighboring Minnesota.

But Kennedy overwhelmed the midwestern liberal known as "the Happy Warrior" by outspending him and staging a Kennedy invasion of Wisconsin that included Jackie, who actually hated this part of politics. One day in a supermarket in Kenosha, Wisconsin, shoppers were startled to hear her breathy voice over the loudspeaker: "Just keep on shopping while I tell you about my husband, John F. Kennedy. He cares deeply about the welfare of his country—please vote for him."[72]

While Humphrey chugged around Wisconsin in a bus, Kennedy flew from event to event in his own airplane, named *Caroline* after his daughter, who was born November 27, 1957. Kennedy also had far more volunteer workers and bought much more television time. "I feel like an independent merchant competing against a chain store,"[73] Humphrey complained.

Kennedy bloodied Humphrey but did not deliver a knockout punch, winning with just 56.5 percent of the vote and carrying six of ten districts. But the four districts Kennedy lost were heavily Protestant, raising again the question of whether Americans were ready to vote for a Catholic as president.

West Virginia

The conventional political wisdom of the time was that a Roman Catholic could not be elected president. The only other Catholic to run for the nation's highest office, Democrat Al Smith, lost to Herbert Hoover in 1928, partly because of fears by non-Catholics that U.S. policies would be subject to control by leaders of his church.

Jacqueline Kennedy was one of the most popular first ladies in U.S. history. She became a political asset to her husband because the public loved her.

Kennedy chose to meet the issue head-on in West Virginia, which was 95 percent Protestant. Kennedy used most of a half-hour-long paid telecast to defuse the issue, explaining that he believed in separation of church and state and that a Catholic had to follow his church's beliefs only in religious matters:

> So when any man stands on the steps of the Capitol and takes the oath of office of President, he is swearing to support the separation of church and state; he puts one hand on the Bible and raises the other hand to God as he takes the oath. And if he breaks his oath, he is not only committing a crime against the Constitution, for which the Congress can impeach him—and should impeach him—but he is committing a sin against God.

He then raised his hand as if from an imaginary Bible, lifting it high and repeating softly, "A sin against God, for he has sworn on the Bible."[74] The speech put the issue to rest, but only for the primaries.

Kennedy also outspent Humphrey and had a far better organization, with some nine thousand volunteers working election day. Kennedy won forty-eight of fifty-five counties with nearly 61 percent of the vote to knock Humphrey out of a campaign that had turned bitter.

Humphrey accused the Kennedys of buying the election:

I don't think elections should be bought. Let that sink in deeply—I can't afford to . . . buy an election. Kennedy is the spoiled candidate and he and that young, emotional juvenile Bobby

---

Houston Speech on Religion

John F. Kennedy put the issue of his religion to the test September 12, 1960, in a speech to the Greater Houston Ministerial Association. Invited to speak to Protestant leaders, he vowed that his Roman Catholic affiliation would not affect him as president.

"Because I am a Catholic, and no Catholic has ever been elected President, the real issues in this campaign have been obscured—perhaps deliberately, in some quarters less responsible than this. I believe in an America where the separation of church and state is absolute—where no Catholic prelate would tell the President [should he be Catholic] how to act, and no Protestant minister would tell his parishioners for whom to vote—where no church or church school is granted any public funds or political preference—and where no man is denied public office merely because his religion differs from the President who might appoint him or the people who might elect him.

I believe in an America that is officially neither Catholic, Protestant nor Jewish—where no public official either requests or accepts instructions on public policy from the Pope, the National Council of Churches or any other ecclesiastical source—where no religious body seeks to impose its will directly or indirectly upon the general populace or the public acts of its officials—and where religious liberty is so indivisible that an act against one church is treated as an act against all.

I am not the Catholic candidate for President. I am the Democratic Party's candidate for President who happens also to be a Catholic. I do not speak for my church on public matters—and the church does not speak for me."

John F. Kennedy campaigns in West Virginia. Kennedy used the primary race in that state to ease fears of non-Catholics that his first allegiance would be not to his country but to the pope and other leaders of his faith.

[Robert Kennedy] are spending with wild abandon. Anybody who gets in the way of papa's pet is going to be destroyed. I don't seem to recall anybody giving the Kennedy family—father, mother, sons or daughters—the privilege of deciding our party's nominee.[75]

Humphrey's uncharacteristically bitter statement summed up the anti-Kennedy feeling that existed even among Democrats. His father was not well liked, and many resented Kennedy's wealth and his use of his family to campaign.

The Convention

The Democratic convention in Los Angeles, California, was a Kennedy triumph. He had won all seven primaries he entered as well as three primaries by write-in, eliminating doubts about his vote-getting power. Kennedy won 806 votes on the first ballot to secure the nomination.

The only convention surprise was his choice for vice president—Lyndon Baines Johnson. The two Senate colleagues had never been close, but the selection of the Texan balanced the ticket geographically and politically. Johnson would help win votes in the South and West, and he was believed to be more conservative than Kennedy.

On July 15, in his nationally televised speech to accept the nomination, Kennedy introduced his campaign theme:

We stand on the edge of a New Frontier—the frontier of the 1960's— a frontier of unknown opportunities and perils—a frontier of unfulfilled hopes and threats. Beyond that frontier are uncharted areas of science and space, unsolved problems of peace and war, unconquered pockets of ignorance and prejudice, unanswered questions of poverty and surplus.[76]

Like Woodrow Wilson's New Freedom, Franklin D. Roosevelt's New Deal, and Harry S Truman's Fair Deal, the New Frontier was a catchphrase designed to sum up the candidate's ideas. Kennedy vowed to "get the country moving again"[77] by dealing with unemployment, the threat of communism, and other problems.

The General Election

In the general election, Kennedy had to conquer his second political deficit—his youth. His Republican opponent, Richard Milhous Nixon, was only four years older at forty-seven but had gained stature in two terms as vice president under Dwight D. Eisenhower. The retiring president disparagingly referred to Kennedy as "that boy" and even former Democratic president Truman questioned whether he had the maturity and experience for the job.

Kennedy defeated that issue and, many believe, won the election because of the impression he made in four nationally televised debates with Nixon. By 1960 nearly 90 percent of American homes had television, and between 65 and 70 million people would watch the debates. Nixon's failure to realize the impact on the election of television, a mass medium only a little more than a decade old, was a serious miscalculation that cost him dearly.

The opening debate on September 26 in Chicago was the most important because it was the first time voters viewed the two candidates side by side. Kennedy, looking fit and handsome despite his many ongoing health problems, was a vivid contrast to Nixon, who looked pale, weak, and tired.

Recovering from a knee injury, Nixon had lost weight and his collar hung loosely around his neck. Because he refused to wear makeup, his drooping jowls looked dark because of his heavy beard, even though he had shaved. He also kept turning to Kennedy to deliver his remarks, as if in a real debate, while Kennedy talked directly to the cameras to maintain eye contact with viewers.

A family watches John F. Kennedy during his televised debate against Republican Richard M. Nixon. The good impression Kennedy made on viewers during the four televised debates was a key factor in his victory in the 1960 presidential election.

Kennedy simply looked more appealing to voters. More importantly, he engaged the incumbent vice president on an equal footing and put to rest, for many, the claims that he was too young or inexperienced.

Television cameras have the power to enhance or detract from a person's appearance, and image becomes more important than substance. The camera loved Kennedy. That power was shown in polls taken after the first debate—more people who listened on radio felt Nixon had won, while more people who watched felt Kennedy was victorious.

The last three debates were considered draws, but Nixon never recovered from his

TV Debates

The Making of the President, 1960, *by Theodore H. White, is considered one of the finest books ever written on a presidential campaign. White called the televised debates a "revolution born of the ceaseless American genius in technology" that would "permit the simultaneous gathering of all the tribes of America to ponder their choice between two chieftains in the largest political convocation in the history of man."*

"As one rereads the text [of the first debate], one finds [Nixon], over and over again, scoring excellently against the personal adversary in the hall beside him, yet forgetful of the need to score on the mind of the nation he hoped to lead. . . . Kennedy was calm and nerveless in appearance. The vice president, by contrast, was tense, almost frightened, at turns glowering and, occasionally, haggard-looking to the point of sickness. . . . After the debates there was a quantum jump in the size of Kennedy crowds."

White had also noted the camera's ability to transform Nixon into a somewhat menacing figure when he watched him during an earlier appearance.

"The man on the stand before me in person was a handsome young American—only recently out of the hospital, he was attractively slim, a fine and healthy American, almost an athlete. His face as he spoke to this friendly audience was a smiling one—and Nixon has a broad, almost sunny smile when he is with friends. His is a broad open face and the deep eye wells, the heavy brows, the broad forehead give it a clean, masculine quality. Yet on television, the deep eye wells and the heavy brows cast shadows on the face and his eyes glowered on the screen darkly; when he became rhetorically indignant, the television showed ferocity; when he turned, his apparently thin brush of hair showed in a glimmering widow's peak."

poor showing in the first. A CBS poll conducted after the election by Elmo Roper showed that of 4 million Americans who were decisively influenced by the debates, 3 million decided to vote for Kennedy. And Kennedy would win the popular vote by a scant 114,673 votes—34,221,344 (49.72 percent) to 34,106,671 (49.55 percent)—although his electoral college margin was 303 to 219.

Earl Mazo, national political editor of the *New York Herald-Tribune,* wrote after the election: "My own view, based on an analysis of surveys and polls I consider reliable and on a first-hand acquaintanceship with much of the campaign and its participants, is that if there had been no debates on television, Nixon would have been elected President."[78]

Another major event in the election was the October 12 arrest of Martin Luther King Jr., who had tried to integrate a restaurant in Atlanta. At the urging of his staff, Kennedy telephoned King's wife, Coretta, on October 25 to assure her of his support, and his brother Robert helped get the crusading civil rights leader freed on bail.

Kennedy, not known before as a leader in civil rights issues, gained a huge number of black votes with that gesture. King's father had been supporting Nixon, but he now switched to Kennedy "because this man was willing to wipe the tears from my daughter [-in-law's] eyes. I've got a suitcase of votes and I'm going to take them to Mr. Kennedy and drop them in his lap."[79]

A Rousing Inaugural

The nation's thirty-fifth president was inaugurated on January 20, 1961. Washing-ton was cloaked in eight inches of snow from a rare snowstorm the day before; soldiers had worked through the night to clear city streets for the big day. Kennedy, trim and youthful, was a stark contrast to Eisenhower, who, at seventy, was the oldest president ever to serve.

Despite the cold weather, Kennedy took the oath without wearing either a coat or a hat, once again masking the health problems that still beset him. Although he complained that his speech was not as good as that of Thomas Jefferson, a figure he revered, Kennedy delivered one of the most stirring inaugurals in history, touching the hearts and minds of millions of Americans.

He ended by calling for their help in perhaps the most famous line he ever delivered: "And so, my fellow Americans: ask not what your country can do for you—ask what you can do for your country."[80]

A Poor Start

Kennedy had hoped to re-create the legendary legislative success of Franklin D. Roosevelt, who, in 1932, pushed through a series of key measures in his first hundred days in office. In just three months, Kennedy sent Congress thirty-nine messages and letters filled with proposals to revive the economy, improve health and medical care for the elderly and poor, aid education, generate new housing and community development, and help struggling farmers.

Kennedy, however, had mixed success in Congress. Although his party held a majority in the House of Representatives, 101 of the 261 Democratic members were southerners, many of whom opposed his social welfare proposals.

John F. Kennedy takes the oath of office to become the nation's thirty-fifth president on January 20, 1961. Jacqueline (far left), wearing one of the fashionable hats she became known for during her husband's presidency, watches proudly as her husband fulfills his dream of becoming president.

The worst thing that happened to Kennedy early in his presidency was the disastrous attempt by Cuban patriots to invade their native land to overthrow communist dictator Fidel Castro, who had come to power in 1959 by defeating Fulgencio Batista, the U.S.-supported dictator. The Cubans who took part in the invasion were called "exiles" because their fierce opposition to Castro's communist regime led them to leave their native land. In 1960 the United States was enforcing an economic embargo against Cuba, and Eisenhower, shortly before leaving office January 3, had cut off diplomatic relations with Cuba.

Under Eisenhower's direction, the Central Intelligence Agency (CIA) had helped the exiles plan the secret invasion. Kennedy did not learn about the controversial proposal until after his election, when Eisenhower briefed him on the plan and other sensitive issues. The first major decision Kennedy had to make was whether to allow the invasion to proceed.

Kennedy had always been a staunch "cold warrior," eager to challenge the Communists whenever possible. He had his doubts about the plan, but CIA director Allen Dulles, a holdover from the Eisenhower administration, and other top military advisers assured him it would succeed.

The young president had named to his cabinet young men, including his brother Robert as attorney general, who would go on to be collectively nicknamed "the Best and the Brightest." But the new, inexperienced team did not perform very well on Cuba. Neither did Kennedy, who displayed the youth and inexperience that had worried some voters during the campaign. He decided to approve the invasion because he relied on Dulles and others who were, presumably, wiser as well as older.

On April 17 about 1,500 Cuban exiles left their base in Nicaragua to invade Cuba, wading ashore from boats at a spot called the Bay of Pigs. But Castro was ready

for the invasion, which was really not so secret after all—U.S. newspapers had been running stories for several months speculating about an invasion. Castro's troops quickly defeated the exiles, killing 115 invaders and capturing 1,189 other exiles; about 150 of the invaders either did not land or escaped.

Before long it was obvious that the small band of exiles was being badly hammered by Castro's well-prepared defenders, and U.S. military advisers urged intervention in the form of aerial support and, eventually, troops. The military, in fact, had always felt that such help would be necessary.

The advisers never shared this assessment with Kennedy because they had feared he would cancel the invasion rather than put American lives at risk. Dulles and others simply assumed that Kennedy, as commander in chief, would authorize the crucial air support when the need became apparent.

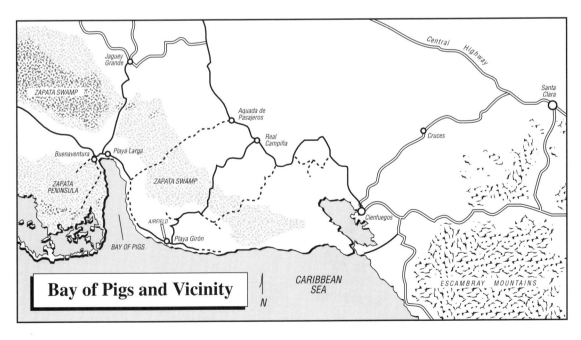

Bay of Pigs and Vicinity

Fidel Castro, the communist dictator who came to power in Cuba in 1959. Castro dealt President Kennedy a major foreign affairs defeat in 1961 with the Bay of Pigs incident.

When the president refused to commit American resources, Castro scored a huge personal and propaganda victory over the United States. He imprisoned the surviving exiles, who were eventually freed on Christmas Eve 1962, in exchange for $53 million in medical supplies, baby food, medical equipment, and similar nonembargoed supplies that were privately donated. No government funds were used for the ransom.

Kennedy shouldered the blame in a news conference. "There's an old saying," he said, "that victory has a hundred fathers and defeat is an orphan. I am the responsible officer for the government and that is quite obvious."[81]

The young president had learned a bitter lesson: Never blindly trust predictions from people you did not know well.

"How could I have been so far off base? All my life I've known better than to depend on the experts. How could have I been so stupid, to let them go ahead,"[82] he told his aides after the military disaster.

6 JFK and the Challenge of Communism

In his first State of the Union message on January 30, 1961, President John F. Kennedy said: "On the Presidential coat of arms, the American eagle holds in his right talon the olive branch, while in his left he holds a bundle of arrows. We intend to give equal attention to both."[83]

With the Bay of Pigs, Kennedy quickly discovered how difficult it is to balance those conflicting desires: to promote peace while at the same time being ready to defend the nation and its policies. It was a fine line that Kennedy would walk during confrontations with Soviet leader Nikita Khrushchev, the Cuban missile crisis, talks on nuclear arms, and communist aggression in Southeast Asia.

The Challenge of the Cold War

The Cold War began when World War II ended.

A primary issue in the Cold War was Germany, the defeated European aggressor in the war. By agreement among the victorious allies in the immediate aftermath of the fighting, the country was divided into four zones for administrative purposes. In 1949, however, the Soviet Union refused to surrender control of its sector and set up a puppet state, which it called the German Democratic Republic (East Germany). The portions administered by the other allies—the United States, England, and France—became the Federal Republic of Germany (West Germany). Berlin, the German capital, lay within East Germany but was occupied jointly by the four former allies.

Communists also took over whole nations, including Czechoslovakia, Hungary, and Poland. The Soviet Union wanted these nations, now known as the Soviet bloc, as a geographic buffer against Western Europe. And in Asia in 1949, Mao Tse-tung led communists to victory in China. Other communist-led takeover attempts occurred during the 1950s and 1960s in other countries in the Far East as well as in Latin America and in Africa.

Although allies during World War II, the United States and the Soviet Union became bitter enemies afterward as the Soviets began forcing their communist form of government on other countries.

The Cold War was based on the opposing ideologies of the two superpowers that emerged after World War II. Americans believed in a democratic government and a capitalistic economic system, one based on private ownership of property and minimal government control. Communism is a totalitarian form of government in which the state owns and controls all segments of the economy.

It was called "the Cold War" because it usually did not involve combat. The weapons were diplomatic measures, propaganda, economic and military aid to other countries, and the threat of nuclear war.

Nikita Khrushchev

Only a few months after the Bay of Pigs fiasco, Kennedy had a chance to redeem himself in a head-to-head confrontation with Nikita Khrushchev, the short, bald Soviet premier who personified the communist menace. Khrushchev once boasted: "We will bury you. Your grandchildren will live under communism."[84]

During the June 3–4 meeting in Vienna, Austria, a belligerent Khrushchev tried to intimidate the U.S. president who was many years his junior. He was defiant on issues and warned Kennedy he might soon deny Western nations access to Berlin. A shaken Kennedy said afterward:

I've got two problems. First to figure out why he did it, and in such a hostile way. And second, to figure out what we can do about it. I think the first part is pretty easy to explain. Obviously he did it because of the Bay of Pigs. I think he thought anyone so callow as to get into a mess like that was dumb, and anybody who got into it and then couldn't see it through had no guts. So he just beat hell out of me. So I've got a terrible problem if he thinks I'm inexperienced and have no guts. Until we remove those ideas we won't get anywhere with him so we have to act.[85]

Kennedy Responds

Kennedy returned home realizing he had to act forcefully to show Khrushchev that he and the nation he governed were not

President Kennedy and Nikita Khrushchev. The short, bald Soviet leader emerged victorious from his first meeting with the young U.S. leader in 1961 in Vienna, Austria, but Kennedy would prevail in later confrontations with the tough-talking communist.

Jackie the Star

The only positive thing to come out of the trip to Europe in June 1961 to meet with Nikita Khrushchev was the emergence of Jacqueline Kennedy as a bona fide international star. She drew rave reviews for her elegance, intelligence, and charm. In A Hero for Our Time: An Intimate Story of the Kennedy Years, *biographer Ralph G. Martin describes Khrushchev's response to the first lady.*

"The 250 guests [at a banquet] were quick to notice how he [Khrushchev] moved his chair even closer to her during dinner. When he told her that the Soviet Ukraine had more teachers than the czarist Ukraine, she said, 'Oh, Mr. Chairman, don't bore me with statistics.' He laughed. When she talked about the dogs in space, he promised to send her one. Khrushchev thought her long, pin-beaded white gown was 'beautiful.' When photographers asked him to pose shaking hands with the President, he pointed at Mrs. Kennedy and said, 'I'd rather shake hands with her.'"

afraid to challenge communism in Berlin or anywhere else in the world. He did so in a July 25 telecast:

> West Berlin has become—as never before—the great testing place of Western courage and will, a focal point where our solemn commitments . . . and Soviet ambitions now meet in basic confrontation. I want to talk frankly with you tonight about the first steps that we shall take. These actions will require sacrifice on the part of many of our citizens. We intend to have a wider choice than humiliation or all-out nuclear action. . . . If that should require more men, or more taxes, or more controls, or other new powers, I shall not hesitate to ask for them. . . . The immediate threat to free men is in West Berlin. . . . An attack upon that city will be regarded as an attack upon us all. We cannot separate its safety from our own.[86]

Kennedy asked for a $3.25-billion hike in defense spending, manpower increases in the armed forces, a tripling of draft calls, and authorization to call up reservists. The new funds were in addition to his January budget request for an additional $3 billion in military spending.

Two decades earlier in *Why England Slept,* Kennedy had argued it was harder for a democratic nation to increase military spending than it was for a totalitarian state. But mail to the White House ran more than 100 to 1 in his support, and a Gallup poll showed more than 67 percent of Americans were willing to fight to keep Berlin free. Congress quickly gave the president what he wanted.

During his brief presidency, Kennedy increased defense spending by $17 billion, presiding over what was then the largest military and naval buildup in the nation's history. It was a response to the Soviet Union, which was also escalating defense spending.

While Eisenhower had concentrated on nuclear missiles, Kennedy built a more balanced, flexible strategic force of air, sea, and ground power—one that could cope with a variety of military needs and included nuclear submarines that could launch missiles from anywhere.

Berlin

The Soviets swiftly answered. Khrushchev liked to brag, "When I want the West to scream, I squeeze in Berlin."[87] Berlin, however, was a problem for Khrushchev because it was an escape hatch for people fleeing the communism of East Germany and other Soviet bloc nations. In July 1961 more than 30,000 people fled to West Berlin, and 16,500 escaped to freedom in the first ten days of August.

On August 13 sirens blared as East German soldiers began erecting a barricade along the twenty-seven-mile perimeter between the city's two halves. At first made of wood and barbed wire, the Berlin Wall gradually became a fortification of concrete and bricks to keep citizens from leaving.

To emphasize the U.S. commitment to Berlin, Kennedy ordered a 350-truck convoy of 1,700 troops to drive to Berlin. The trucks were held up for a tense 14 hours at the first checkpoint in East Germany, but they were eventually allowed to proceed.

Kennedy acted quickly because he was worried that the Soviets might try to block land access to their sector as they had done in 1948 when Truman was president. In 1948 the United States had responded with the Berlin airlift, a massive daily aerial transfusion of tons of fuel, food, and other necessities that kept residents supplied until the blockade ended May 12, 1949.

On September 1, 1961, the Soviets resumed nuclear testing, breaking an agreement that had been in effect for several years. During the next two months they detonated forty bombs, releasing radioactive material into the atmosphere. On September 15 the United States resumed underground testing but conducted no atmospheric tests until the next March. Tensions between the two nations had never been higher.

Other Trouble Spots

Berlin and Cuba were the Cold War hot spots that created the most dangerous situations during Kennedy's presidency, but the two ideologies were also clashing in many other parts of the world. Because he was worried that communism would spread to Latin America, on March 13, 1961, Kennedy announced a new foreign aid program:

> I have called on all people of the [Western] hemisphere to join in a new Alliance for Progress—Alianza para Progreso—a vast cooperative effort unparalleled in magnitude and nobility of purpose, to satisfy the basic needs of people for homes, work and land, health and schools . . . techo, trabajo y tierra, salud y escuela.[88]

Kennedy wanted to strengthen the economies of Latin American nations to prevent communism from taking over. The program included funds for regional marketing, national planning, commodity stabilization, education, and technical training.

Both sides used foreign aid liberally to buy the loyalty of other countries. Kennedy, for example, expanded the Food-for-Peace program to many developing nations.

"Ich Bin ein Berliner"

John F. Kennedy's speech in West Berlin June 26, 1963, marked one of the most dramatic, emotional moments of his life. His salute to citizens of West Berlin for keeping the flame of democracy alive in the heart of a communist stronghold rang loud and clear throughout the world.

"Today, in the world of freedom, the proudest boast is 'Ich bin ein Berliner.'

There are many people in the world who really don't understand, or say they don't, what is the great issue between the free world and the Communist world. Let them come to Berlin. There are some who say that communism is the wave of the future. Let them come to Berlin. And there are some who say in Europe and elsewhere we can work with the Communists. Let them come to Berlin. And there are even a few who say that it is true that communism is an evil system, but it permits us to make economic progress. Lass' Sie nach Berlin kommen. Let them come to Berlin.

Freedom has many difficulties and democracy is not perfect, but we have never had to put a wall up to keep our people in, to prevent them from leaving us. I want to say, on behalf of my countrymen, who live many miles away on the other side of the Atlantic, who are far distant from you, that they take the greatest pride that they have been able to share with you, even from a distance, the story of the last 18 years. I know of no town, no city, that has been besieged for 18 years that still lives with the vitality and the force, and the hope and the determination of the city of West Berlin. While the wall is the most obvious and vivid demonstration of the failures of the Communist system, for all the world to see, we take no satisfaction in it, for it is, as your Mayor has said, an offense not only against history but an offense against humanity, separating families, dividing husbands and wives and brothers and sisters, and dividing a people who wish to be joined together."

During his first eighteen months in office, the United States shipped more food abroad than it had in ten years of massive relief to victims of World War I. "It is hard for any nation to focus on an external or subversive threat," Kennedy said, "when its energies are drained in daily combat with the forces of poverty and despair." [89]

This economic warfare, which also included funds for military expenditures, was used extensively in Africa, where new nations that had emerged in the late 1950s and early 1960s from the breakup of European colonies were ripe for communist takeover.

A similar propaganda weapon, one that would do a great deal of good, was the Peace Corps. Tens of thousands of idealistic volunteers spread across the world to help less-developed countries learn to be self-sufficient.

One of the pictures taken by U-2 spy planes that touched off the Cuban missile crisis. The photos were evidence that Cuba had nuclear weapons capable of striking the United States.

Cuban Missile Crisis

On Tuesday, October 16, 1962, presidential assistant McGeorge Bundy interrupted the president while he was eating breakfast to show him pictures taken high over Cuba by a U-2 spy plane. The photos would push the United States and the Soviet Union to the brink of nuclear war.

The pictures proved that Soviet technicians were helping Cuba build facilities that could launch nuclear missiles, something the United States had suspected. U.S. intelligence estimated that, if launched, the missiles could hit targets in half the nation and kill 80 million Americans.

Khrushchev, still doubting Kennedy's courage, had placed the missiles there to test the young president. "I guess this is the week I earn my salary," [90] Kennedy said.

The president had learned from the Bay of Pigs fiasco that during a crisis he needed to surround himself with people he trusted. The day Kennedy saw the photos, he organized twenty-one top aides and officials into the Executive Committee of the National Security Council (ExComm). The group included Secretary of State Dean Rusk, Defense Secretary Robert McNamara, new Central Intelligence Agency director John McCone, and presidential advisers George Ball, McGeorge Bundy, Theodore Sorensen, and General Maxwell Taylor. His brother Robert would emerge as the group's most important member.

ExComm considered every option, from invasion to a nuclear strike, to knock out the missile sites. But Kennedy, worried that the Soviets might respond with nuclear weapons, favored more conservative tactics. Gradually, over several days, Kennedy and his advisers agreed on a naval blockade to force the Russians to remove the missiles. It was called a "quarantine" to make it sound less menacing.

To keep the crisis secret, the president honored a commitment to campaign that Friday in Chicago for Democratic candidates. On Saturday morning he returned to Washington, covering up the real reason for his return by saying he had a cold. After arriving in Washington, Kennedy helped finalize plans and scheduled a radio and television address for Monday night.

That night Kennedy told America about the missiles:

> This secret, swift, and extraordinary buildup of Communist missiles—in an area well known to have a special and historical relationship to the United States and the nations of the Western Hemisphere, in violation of Soviet assurances, and in defiance of American and hemispheric policy—this sudden, clandestine decision to station strategic weapons for the first time outside of Soviet soil—is a deliberately provoca-

tive and unjustified change in the status quo which cannot be accepted by this country, if our courage and our commitments are ever to be trusted again by either friend or foe.[91]

Kennedy demanded the missiles be removed within two days; if this did not happen, he promised, the United States would begin a naval blockade of offensive military shipments to Cuba. He warned of further military action if the missiles were not dismantled. Kennedy also said he would consider any missile attack by Cuba anywhere in the Western Hemisphere an attack by the Soviet Union—and the United States would retaliate the same way against the Soviets.

> My fellow citizens, let no one doubt that this is a difficult and dangerous effort on which we have set out. No one can see precisely what course it will take or what costs or casualties will be incurred. Many months of sacrifice and self-discipline lie ahead—months in which our patience and our will will be

President Kennedy and his brother, Attorney General Robert F. Kennedy, confer during the Cuban missile crisis. His brother became the president's most trusted adviser during this perilous period in U.S. history.

tested—months in which many threats and denunciations will keep us aware of our dangers. But the greatest danger of all would be to do nothing.[92]

Before the speech Secretary of State Rusk personally delivered the same message to Soviet ambassador Anatoly Dobrynin. As 180 U.S. ships moved into position around Cuba and U.S. forces massed on the eastern seaboard for a possible invasion, which was one of the options, the president awaited the Soviet response.

The entire world was frightened about the possibility of a nuclear conflagration that could be so devastating it could wipe out civilization. But on Wednesday, October 24, the crisis eased when the Soviets halted a half dozen ships on their way to Cuba. "We're eyeball to eyeball and I think the other fellow just blinked,"[93] said Rusk.

On Friday, October 26, the Soviets allowed a ship to be boarded and searched before proceeding to Cuba. That night Khrushchev sent a letter by teletype agree-

Peace Corps

In John F. Kennedy and a New Generation, *David Burner argues that the Peace Corps was one of the most effective programs President John F. Kennedy devised to help win support around the world for the United States.*

"The Peace Corps was the American agency that had the most enduring effect on Africa as well as on most of the Third World. The 100,000 volunteers who have served in the Corps [up to 1988] are one of the Kennedy Administration's most enduring legacies.

If viewed skeptically, the Kennedy volunteers and their successors might seem to be little more than warriors in the Cold War, compounding Americanism and capitalism and containment of communism. In fact they were road surveyors, nurses, agricultural technicians, engineers, and teachers. These specialties were always at the core of the experience because literacy correlated so well with improved living conditions. Peace corps members rarely argued for United States foreign policy; but by respecting the cultural integrity of their host countries, they built a goodwill that had undoubted political usefulness. If this was more Kennedy counterinsurgency, it wore a velvet glove. Peace corps service was in vivid response to this call of the inaugural: 'Ask not what your country can do for you—ask what you can do for your country.' The corps, as one history says, 'came to epitomize the ideals and hope that so many young people invested in Kennedy.'"

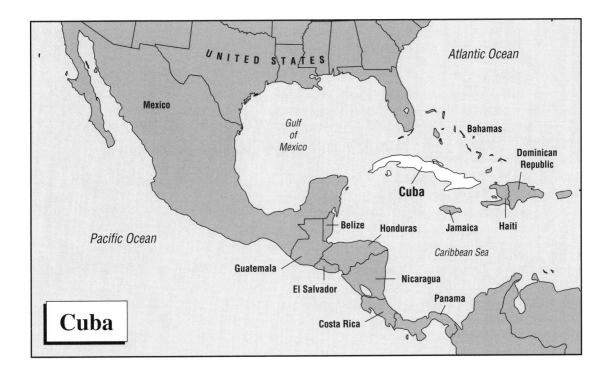

Cuba

ing to remove the missiles if the United States pledged not to invade Cuba. The next day, however, the Soviet leader sent a second, tougher communiqué saying he would remove the missiles only if the United States withdrew missiles it had in Turkey.

Kennedy met with ExComm about the two contradictory notes. Robert Kennedy suggested responding to the first note and disregarding the second. The president agreed; on Saturday, October 27, he sent Khrushchev a message agreeing to the terms in his first note. The Soviets were warned that if they did not respond favorably within twenty-four hours, the United States would take unspecified further military action.

The answer came the next morning: The Soviet Union would dismantle the missiles. Kennedy had won an important Cold War victory.

Nuclear Test Ban

The fact that the United States and the Soviet Union had teetered on the brink of war sobered both Kennedy and Khrushchev. In agreeing to end the crisis, Khrushchev struck a conciliatory note: "We should like to continue the exchange of views on the prohibition of atomic and thermonuclear weapons, general disarmament, and other problems relating to the relaxation of international tension."[94]

For years the United States and the Soviet Union had held talks on limiting nuclear arms, but they had never been able to agree on anything except a test ban, which both sides had now broken. Kennedy realized it was time to slow the arms race, which had resulted in both sides stockpiling enough weapons to destroy the world many times over. He began to

Seated next to President Kennedy is Defense Secretary Robert S. McNamara, one of the so-called "Best and Brightest" who served in Kennedy's Cabinet. The picture is of a meeting during the Cuban missile crisis.

consider the problem and communicated with Khrushchev both directly and through third parties.

On June 10, 1963, Kennedy used a commencement address at American University in Washington, D.C., to propose a new "world peace" to ease the nuclear threat:

> What kind of peace do I mean? What kind of peace do we seek? Not a Pax Americana enforced on the world by American weapons of war. Not the peace of the grave or the security of the slave. I am talking about genuine peace, the kind of peace that makes life on earth worth living, the kind that enables men and nations to grow and to hope and to build a better life for their children—not merely peace for Americans but peace for all men and women—not merely peace in our time but peace for all time.

> I speak of peace because of the new face of war. Total war makes no sense in an age when great powers can maintain large and relatively invulnerable

nuclear forces and refuse to surrender without resort to those forces. It makes no sense in an age when a single nuclear weapon contains almost ten times the explosive force delivered by all the allied air forces in the Second World War. It makes no sense in an age when the deadly poisons produced by a nuclear exchange would be carried by wind and water and soil and seed to the far corners of the globe and to generations yet unborn.[95]

Kennedy announced the two nations would meet to work out terms on a nuclear test ban. He also said the United States would quit atmospheric testing and would do so as long as other nations did.

Although he asked Americans to adopt a new, more understanding attitude toward the Soviet Union, he stressed that his country still considered the Soviet version of Marx and Lenin's philosophy of communism "profoundly repugnant as a negation of personal freedom and dignity."[96]

During a visit to Europe in June, Kennedy felt he needed to reaffirm the U.S.

commitment to defending freedom. Kennedy did this in Berlin on June 26, 1963. In what may have been his greatest speech, he thanked Berliners for the hardships they had endured to keep freedom alive. "All free men," Kennedy said, "wherever they may live, are citizens of Berlin, and, therefore, as a free man, I take pride in the words: 'Ich bin ein Berliner.'"[97] Several hundred thousand people who listened cheered wildly in one of the most triumphant moments of his presidency.

Despite the militancy of his Berlin speech, talks with the Soviets went smooth-ly. An agreement known as the Limited Nuclear Test Ban Treaty was worked out, and the Senate approved it in September.

The treaty banned the testing of nuclear weapons in outer space, the atmosphere, or in the oceans. It was important because the treaty came 13 years and 336 nuclear explosions after the world's first nuclear bomb devastated Hiroshima, Japan, and the tests that had begun to contaminate the environment with radioactive fallout.

When Kennedy signed the bill on October 7, he announced that a "hot line"

President Kennedy addresses a crowd of hundreds of thousands of Germans who gathered in West Berlin June 26, 1963, to hear his message of hope and freedom. They cheered wildly when the president declared, "Ich bin ein Berliner (I am a citizen of Berlin)."

had been in effect since August 30 to lower the risk of war by allowing instant communication between leaders of the two nations during a crisis. He also said the United States would sell 65 million bushels of wheat to Russia, which had had a poor harvest. The day after signing the bill, Kennedy spoke positively about the event.

> Yesterday, a shaft of light cut into the darkness. For the first time an agreement has been reached on bringing the forces of nuclear destruction under international control. It offers all the world a welcome sign of hope. It is not a victory for one side—it is a victory for mankind. It ended the tests which befouled the air of all men and all nations.[98]

Kennedy had achieved the first thaw in the Cold War.

Southeast Asia

Although Kennedy was far more concerned about events in Cuba and Berlin, the Cold War struggle in Southeast Asia would have more significant long-term consequences for America.

In 1954 nationalist and communist Vietnamese forces led by Ho Chi Minh defeated French troops in the decisive battle of Dien Bien Phu. The Geneva Accords worked out by the United Nations (UN) split Indochina, which France had ruled as a colony since the 1900s, into Vietnam, Laos, and Cambodia. The UN divided Vietnam into southern and northern halves along the seventeenth parallel, with North Vietnam going to Ho's communist faction.

The UN also scheduled an internationally supervised election to reunite Vietnam in 1956.

The harsh colonial policies of the French had pushed many Indochinese toward communism, and an armed struggle began for political control of the new nations. When Kennedy became president, the worst fighting was in Laos, where a UN-brokered cease-fire had been broken. Because Kennedy believed in the domino theory, that if one country fell to communism other nearby nations also would, the United States funneled $300 million to the government of Laos to resist military aggression by the communist Pathet Lao.

The United States came close to military intervention in Laos. But a new cease-

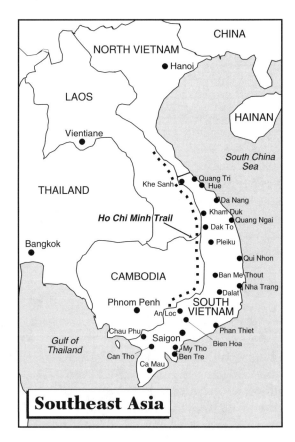

Southeast Asia

U.S. soldiers in South Vietnam in 1962. Although President Kennedy increased the number of U.S. soldiers in South Vietnam during his presidency, before his death he had stated he wanted to disengage from the conflict and had already begun ordering withdrawals of some troops.

fire was agreed on in May, and in 1962 both sides accepted a coalition government.

South Vietnam

The focus then shifted to South Vietnam, where leader Ngo Dinh Diem refused to allow the 1956 national election ordered by the Geneva Accords. Communists in North Vietnam had wanted the elections, and their supporters in South Vietnam began a civil war to overthrow Ngo in 1958.

The United States had fruitlessly spent some $3 billion trying to help the French retain control of Indochina, but from 1955 on U.S. officials financed 100 percent of South Vietnam's government operations in another attempt to keep it democratic. Despite the aid, by 1962 Ho's Vietcong had taken control of much of South Vietnam.

General Maxwell Taylor and White House aide Walt Rostow now advised Kennedy to send a small number of U.S. military advisers to strengthen South Vietnam's army. When Kennedy came into office only two thousand U.S. soldiers were stationed in Vietnam, but by the time he was assassinated that number had increased to sixteen thousand.

Ngo Overthrown

When Vice President Lyndon B. Johnson visited South Vietnam in 1961, he hailed Ngo as the "Winston Churchill of South Asia."[99] It was a title he did not deserve. A Roman Catholic in a country that was more than 90 percent Buddhist, Ngo presided over a corrupt, repressive government that did little to help the nation's millions of peasants.

Ngo opposed U.S.-backed social reforms such as giving land to poor peasants who had none or very little and increased health and education services. Unpopular with most South Vietnamese, Ngo stayed in power only because of U.S. support. Ho, on the other hand, was a folk hero to many in both halves of Vietnam for his leadership in driving out the French.

How the United States Was Involved in the Ngo Coup

President Kennedy denied U.S. involvement in the coup that resulted in the death of the Ngo Dinh Diem. But in President Kennedy, *Richard Reeves says U.S. representatives—with Kennedy's knowledge—fostered a climate that allowed the coup to proceed.*

According to Reeves, on November 6, in a private cable to the president from South Vietnam, Ambassador Henry Cabot Lodge Jr. wrote:

"There is no doubt that the coup was a Vietnamese and a popular affair, which we could neither manage nor stop after it got started and which we could only have influenced with great difficulty. But it is equally certain that the ground in which the coup seed grew into a robust plant was prepared by us and that the coup would not have happened as it did without our preparation."

On May 8, 1963, in the city of Hue, South Vietnamese troops fired into a crowd protesting Ngo's orders not to fly the Buddhist flag. Buddhist demonstrations soon spread to other cities, and on June 11 Buddhist monk Thich Quang Duc committed suicide in Saigon by setting himself on fire. When other monks committed suicide, Madame Nhu, Ngo's sister-in-law, called the incidents "barbecue" and said, "I will be glad to supply the gasoline. Let them burn and we shall clap our hands."[100]

Madame Nhu's comments inflamed many Vietnamese and strengthened feelings against Ngo. On September 3 even Kennedy admitted that Ngo had "gotten out of touch with the people"[101] and needed to change his policies to survive.

Ngo did not survive. On November 1, three weeks before Kennedy's assassination, Ngo and his equally hated brother, Ngo Dinh Nhu, were shot to death in a military takeover. The new South Vietnamese ruler was General Duong "Big" Van Minh.

With ongoing U.S. support, Minh continued to fight the Vietcong in what soon escalated into the Vietnam War, the most divisive conflict in U.S. history and one that would claim the lives of 57,939 Americans.

7 Other Challenges: Civil Rights, Space, the Economy

For most of his career, John F. Kennedy was a political enigma to friend and foe alike. Despite being a Democrat, he did not always act like one, and he was not easily categorized as either a liberal or a conservative.

In foreign affairs Kennedy was very conservative when first elected to Congress, as in his opposition to foreign aid, but his views changed over the years. For example, there were liberal elements in some of his Cold War proposals, such as the Alliance for Progress, which stressed improving living standards of Latin Americans as the best way to oppose communism below the Mexican border.

On domestic issues he generally sided with liberals on social welfare programs, backed labor unions, and supported civil rights. But Kennedy was fiscally conservative and, along with his brother Robert, led the fight against union corruption even though labor was an important backer of the Democratic Party.

In his Senate years, and when he began his quest for the presidency, Kennedy grew closer to mainstream Democratic philosophy and became more liberal. This courting of liberals led some to accuse Kennedy of political expediency, but he maintained it was simply a natural evolution of his thinking.

President Kennedy meets in the White House in 1961 with a delegation of the National Association for the Advancement of Colored People. Civil rights was Kennedy's greatest domestic challenge.

"Some people have their liberalism 'made' by the time they reach their late 20s," he once said almost wistfully. "I didn't. I was caught in cross currents and eddies. It was only later that I got into the stream of things." [102] Biographer David Burner contends that "the swift-moving history of the late fifties and early sixties carried him along, shaping him into a liberal whatever his own reservations." [103]

As president, Kennedy's late-blooming liberalism was most clearly evident in his actions on domestic issues. And it was on the sweeping events of the civil rights movement, which overshadowed every other issue, that he left his greatest mark.

Jump-Starting the Economy

The first item on Kennedy's presidential agenda was to snap the nation out of the 1960 economic recession, the third in a decade (the others occurred in 1953 and 1958), and to reduce 8.1 percent unemployment. On February 21, 1961, he sent Congress a comprehensive economic message with a long list of proposals to rejuvenate the economy. Nearly all passed by the end of June.

They included a temporary thirteen-week supplement of unemployment benefits for nearly 3 million workers plus aid for their children; an increase of 25 cents in the minimum wage (to $1.25 an hour) and coverage for 3.6 million more workers; a hike in Social Security payments, inclusion of 5 million more people, and a lower retirement age of sixty-two; nearly $5 billion for a housing bill to help low- and moderate-income families; and the Area Redevelopment Act to rejuvenate economically depressed areas and retrain unemployed workers. The president also sought legislation to raise farm price supports, start the food stamp program, and speed the flow of federal dollars to existing programs.

The massive infusion of federal dollars revived the economy in his first year, creating jobs in construction, farming, and other sectors. Kennedy summed up the economic recovery in his second State of the Union message on January 11, 1962: "At home we began the year in the valley of recession; we completed it on the high road of recovery and growth. . . . At year's end the economy which Mr. [Nikita] Khrushchev once called a 'stumbling horse' was racing to new records in consumer spending, labor income and industrial production." [104]

In 1961 Kennedy proposed a 7 percent tax credit for business investment in new machinery and equipment and more generous depreciation allowances for new plants and equipment. It passed in 1962, creating an 11 percent cut in business taxes. In 1962 Kennedy also secured passage of the Trade Expansion Act, which gave him the power to end tariffs on some imports to increase U.S. trade with Europe.

Under the Kennedy administration the nation's economic growth rate was 5.7 percent, compared to 2.3 percent under Dwight D. Eisenhower, unemployment fell to 5 percent, and inflation was a low 1.3 percent.

Legislative Failures

During his first two years as president, Kennedy proposed 653 pieces of legislation, about double the rate of Eisenhower,

John F. Kennedy—Liberal

On September 14, 1960, Senator John F. Kennedy accepted the presidential nomination of the country's only avowedly progressive party, the Liberal Party, in New York City. At that time he defined his liberalism.

"What do our opponents mean when they apply to us the label 'Liberal'? If by 'Liberal' they mean, as they want people to believe, someone who is soft in his policies abroad, who is against local government, and who is unconcerned with the taxpayer's dollar, then the record of this party and its members demonstrate that we are not that kind of 'Liberal.' But if by a 'Liberal' they mean someone who looks ahead and not behind, someone who welcomes new ideas without rigid reactions, someone who cares about the welfare of the people—their health, their housing, their schools, their jobs, their civil rights, and their civil liberties—someone who believes we can break through the stalemate and suspicions that grip us in our policies abroad, if that is what they mean by a 'Liberal,' then I'm proud to say I'm a 'Liberal.'

I believe in human dignity as the source of national purpose, in human liberty as the source of national action, in the human heart as the source of national compassion, and in the human mind as the source of our invention and our ideas. It is, I believe, the faith in our fellow citizens as individuals and as people that lies at the heart of the liberal faith. For liberalism is not so much a party creed or set of fixed platform promises as it is an attitude of mind and heart, a faith in man's ability through the experiences of his reason and judgment to increase for himself and his fellow men the amount of justice and freedom and brotherhood which all human life deserves."

and almost half (304) passed. But Congress balked at major proposals such as subsidized medical care for the aged, creation of a Department of Urban Affairs, and increased general aid to education.

Opposing the president on these issues were southern Democrats, who were conservative and often voted with Republicans. Kennedy was especially angry at the defeat of the initial proposal for Medicare, which would have provided health insurance for people sixty-five and older.

Kennedy also lost on his bid to lower taxes to further stimulate the economy, which he proposed in his third and last State of the Union address in January 1963:

President Kennedy also had to deal with the economy, the space race, and other domestic problems.

The cuts would have created a budget deficit the first year of $12.8 billion. But economic advisers had convinced Kennedy that a stronger economy would increase revenue by creating more taxable personal and business income. This theory, known as supply-side economics, was a radical departure from traditional economic thought, which held that governments should hold to balanced budgets.

The tax cut bill passed the House in September but was bottled up in the Senate after Kennedy was killed in November. But as with his civil rights bill, also trapped in the House at his death, and Medicare, it would be approved under his successor, President Lyndon B. Johnson.

The Space Race

It is increasingly clear that our obsolete tax system exerts too heavy a drag on private purchasing power, profits, and employment. I shall propose a permanent reduction in tax rates, which will lower liabilities by $13.5 billion [a tax cut equal to almost 15 percent of the federal budget]. Of this $11 billion results from reducing individual tax rates, which now range between 29 and 91 percent, to a more sensible range of 14 to 65 percent. Two and one half billion dollars results from reducing corporate tax rates from 52 percent—which gives the government today a majority interest in profits—to the permanent pre–Korean war rate of 47 percent.[105]

In the Cold War era, Kennedy, like most elected officials, thought of almost every issue in terms of the challenge of communism. Thus, Kennedy felt the nation had suffered a humiliating defeat April 12, 1961, when Russian cosmonaut Yuri Gagarin became the first man to orbit the earth. On May 5 astronaut Alan Shepard became the first American in space, but it was little consolation—the Soviets had beaten the United States into that new frontier.

Perhaps Kennedy's greatest strength was his ability to inspire his fellow Americans. He did so, challenging the nation to conquer space, in his special message to Congress on May 25, 1961:

If we are to win the battle that is now going on around the world between freedom and tyranny, the dramatic achievements in space which occurred in recent weeks should have made clear to us all, as did the Sputnik in 1957 [when Russia became the first to launch a space satellite], the impact of this adventure on the minds of men everywhere, who are attempting to make a determination of which [ideological] road they should take. . . . I believe we possess all the resources and talents necessary [to win the space race]. But the facts of the matter are that we have never made the national decisions or marshaled the national resources required for such leadership. We have never specified long-range goals on an urgent time schedule, or managed our resources and our time so as to insure their fulfillment.[106]

Why Explore Space?

In an address at Rice University in Houston, Texas, on September 12, 1962, President Kennedy explained why the space program was important.

"We set sail on this new sea because there is new knowledge to be gained, and new rights to be won, and they must be won and used for the progress of all people. For space science, like nuclear science and all technology, has no conscience of its own. Whether it will become a force for good or ill depends on man, and only if the United States occupies a position of pre-eminence can we help decide whether this new ocean will be a sea of peace or a new terrifying theater of war.

But why, some say, the moon? Why choose this as our goal? And they may well ask why climb the highest mountain? Why, 35 years ago, fly the Atlantic? Why does Rice play Texas? We choose to go to the moon. We choose to go to the moon in this decade and do the other things, not because they are easy, but because they are hard, because that goal will serve to organize and measure the best of our energies and skills, because that challenge is one that we are willing to accept, one we are unwilling to postpone, and one which we intend to win, and the others, too.

It is for these reasons that I regard the decision last year to shift our efforts in space from low to high gear as among the most important decisions that will be made during my incumbency in the office of the Presidency."

Kennedy then delighted Congress and the entire nation by boldly setting a goal for the U.S. space program, one that seemed straight out of a science fiction novel:

> I believe that this nation should commit itself . . . before this decade is out, of landing a man on the moon and returning him safely to the earth. No single space project in this period will be more impressive to mankind, or more important for the long-range exploration of space; and none will be so difficult or expensive to accomplish. . . .

> It will not be one man going to the moon—if we make this judgment affirmatively, it will be an entire nation. For all of us must work to put him there.[107]

Kennedy asked for an additional $80 million in funding for the space program as well as another $75 million, most of it to develop a satellite system for worldwide weather observation. Congress approved the expenditures, allowing construction in Florida of the base at Cape Canaveral (renamed Cape Kennedy after the president's death) and the Mission Control Center in Houston. The funding got the space program moving, and on July 20, 1969, Neil Armstrong set foot on the moon to meet Kennedy's timetable.

The president also saw the Soviet's lead in the space race as a sign that U.S. education needed to improve. He increased funding to public schools and created programs to reduce the dropout rate and teach literacy outside of school. His 1963 Higher Education Act produced more aid for colleges in five years than had been granted in the last century.

Civil Rights

On February 12, 1963, the U.S. Civil Rights Commission gave President Kennedy a 246-page report that summed up the progress that African Americans had made in the century since President Abraham Lincoln issued the Emancipation Proclamation. The news was dismal.

The report said African Americans were inheritors of "a freedom more fictional than real," noting that the "legally free Negro citizen was denied the franchise, excluded from public office, assigned to inferior and separate schools, herded into ghettoes, directed to the back of the bus, treated unequally in the courts of justice and segregated in his illness, his worship, and even in his death." But the report also said "the final chapter in the struggle for equality has yet to be written" and pointed out that "more forces are working for the realization of civil rights for all Americans [today] than ever before in history."[108]

A century after being freed as slaves, African Americans were still denied basic rights guaranteed by the Constitution. While Kennedy was president, the civil rights movement exploded, making major strides in waking up Americans to the facts of racism and discrimination in their nation. For the first time in history, Kennedy threw the power of the United States behind this fight for equal rights.

In May 1961 "Freedom Riders" on two public buses were attacked by white racists in Alabama; at Anniston a mob burned a bus and in Birmingham riders were beaten. The thirteen Freedom Riders were black and white members of the Congress of Racial Equality (CORE) who were traveling into southern states to defy local ordi-

Why Kennedy Acted Slowly on Civil Rights

In One Brief Shining Moment: Remembering Kennedy, *longtime friend William Manchester explains why Kennedy attacked racism more slowly at first than African Americans would have liked.*

"[Kennedy was a] typical liberal of his generation and even though it was brave in 1961 just to endorse racial quality before an audience of southern whites he and his brother, the attorney general, felt it would take time. Bobby, in his first speech as Attorney General in Athens, Georgia, on May 6, 1961, said if blacks were not treated equally 'the Department of Justice will act. We will not stand by or be aloof.' Of course, as he and his brother had privately explained to black leaders, these things took *time*. They couldn't expect it all *now*. That was the flaw: the blacks wanted it now. They knew the Kennedys' hearts were in the right place, but they had been listening to promises year after year, and nothing had happened. It had become clear to them that racial prejudice was far more powerful than white liberals realized; that it was impervious to reason; and that if it was to be defeated some people, probably their own people, were going to have to die. The time had come for action—not filing motions, and issuing subpoenas, which is what Bobby meant—but physical action: white flesh against black flesh, black flesh against clubs, police dogs, fire hoses, even bullets. And the vanguard of their crusade was already on the move."

nances mandating segregation of restaurants, restrooms, and waiting rooms. CORE leader James Farmer had been inspired to act by Kennedy's promise of change.

When other riders joined the protest, resulting in more violence, Robert Kennedy sent more than six hundred federal marshals to Montgomery, Alabama, to protect them. The attorney general also petitioned the Interstate Commerce Commission (ICC) to issue regulations desegregating travel fa-

cilities. The ICC complied in September, and when some cities cited local laws as an excuse for noncompliance, the Justice Department threatened federal action to ensure the laws were removed. The crisis over civil rights faded, but only for a while.

At the time of the Freedom Rides, Kennedy was preparing for the most important meeting of his life—the summit in Vienna with Soviet premier Nikita Khrushchev. As the date approached, the Soviets

President Kennedy meets with black leaders in the White House. Fourth from the left is the Rev. Martin Luther King Jr., the era's greatest civil rights leader.

tried to influence world opinion about the United States by claiming that racial problems in America proved that capitalism was not working.

The civil rights movement was a political problem for a president who had narrowly won election and, already looking ahead to the 1964 contest, feared alienating southern voters by moving too quickly. Kennedy wanted to advance slowly on the issue by working with his brother Robert to create positive change through the legal system. The Kennedys also knew how hard it would be to push legislation through Congress because of southern opposition.

Kennedy felt the best way to help African Americans was to ensure that they could vote; in 1960 only 28 percent of southern African Americans were registered to vote. In 1962 Kennedy submitted

two voting rights measures: One outlawed poll taxes, which southern states used to keep poor African Americans from voting, and one exempted citizens with at least a sixth-grade education from literacy tests used to deny blacks the vote. The proposal to abolish the poll tax eventually became the Twenty-Fourth Amendment to the U.S. Constitution, but southerners defeated the second measure.

Starting in 1961, the Justice Department stepped up efforts under existing laws to reduce voter discrimination, filing dozens of lawsuits. The Justice Department also served notice that it would start enforcing the landmark 1954 Supreme Court decision that outlawed segregation in public schools.

The president issued executive orders barring segregation and discrimination in the armed forces reserves and federal government; encouraged federal agencies to hire more African Americans; and formed the President's Committee on Equal Employment Opportunity.

But those tactics would take time, and the nation's 21 million African Americans were tired of waiting. "For years now," said the Reverend Martin Luther King Jr., "I have heard the word 'Wait!' It rings in the ear of every Negro with piercing familiarity. This 'Wait' has always meant 'Never.'" [109]

Black Protests

The modern battle for civil rights began in 1955, when a brave woman named Rosa Parks refused to give up her seat on a bus in racially segregated Montgomery, Alabama. Her arrest sparked demonstrations and a year-long boycott of the bus system by African Americans. The Supreme Court ruled the next year that racial segregation in businesses was unconstitutional.

The battle continued in 1957, when King, who had gained national prominence for leading the demonstrations, founded the Southern Christian Leadership Conference (SCLC). The SCLC began a series of peaceful protests throughout the south to win such simple rights for African Americans as eating at the same lunch counter with whites.

The tactics King adopted were based on the philosophy of nonviolence advanced by Mohandas Gandhi of India when he led the fight to free his nation from British rule. "We must love our white brothers no matter what they do to us," King said. Historian Robert Kelley explains how King educated his followers into this powerful philosophy:

Mass indoctrination in nonviolence now began; black southerners were taught what it meant and how to use it. Almost nightly in the black churches, which were the heart of black culture, there were lectures and films on techniques and tactics; on accepting appalling white abuse, instructions on sitting in, holding one's place, marching and demonstrating, all without undignified shouting back at white taunts, without physical response. "If cursed, do not curse back. If struck, do not strike back, but evidence love and goodwill at all times. If another person is being molested, do not arise to go to his defense, but pray for the oppressor." King meant it. Indeed, it was his awesome integrity, as well as his fluent rolling phrases and his charisma, the aura of being touched by destiny, that allowed him for a decade to hold millions of people to this incredible course of self-denial, faith, and love. [110]

While Kennedy was president, such nonviolent protests increased in number, forcing him to act quickly on civil rights.

James Meredith

The next civil rights crisis came in September 1962, when James Meredith, a young air force veteran inspired by Kennedy's inaugural address, tried to enroll at the University of Mississippi. Mississippi was a state in which only sixty thousand of its 1 million blacks could vote because of discriminatory voting laws and only whites could attend its public university.

When he was refused admission because of his race on January 21, 1961, Meredith filed a lawsuit, which he won a year later. Despite the court order, Meredith was refused admission several days in a row starting on September 25. The president ordered three hundred federal marshals to Oxford, Mississippi, to force the university to admit Meredith.

On the night of September 30, after Meredith had been escorted onto the campus by armed marshals, Kennedy ex-

Civil Rights Address

On June 11, 1963, President Kennedy delivered a national address on civil rights. It was one of the most forceful, eloquent expressions on behalf of equality ever delivered by a president.

"We are confronted primarily with a moral issue. It is as old as the scriptures and is as clear as the American Constitution.

The heart of the question is whether all Americans are to be afforded equal rights and equal opportunities, whether we are going to treat our fellow Americans as we want to be treated. If an American, because his skin is dark, cannot eat lunch in a restaurant open to the public, if he cannot send his children to the best public school available, if he cannot vote for the public officials who will represent him, if, in short, he cannot enjoy the full and free life which all of us want, then who among us would be content to have the color of his skin changed and stand in his place? Who among us would then be content with the counsels of patience and delay?

One hundred years of delay have passed since President Lincoln freed the slaves, yet their heirs, their grandsons, are not fully free. They are not yet freed from the bonds of injustice. They are not yet freed from social and economic oppression. And this Nation, for all its hopes and all its boasts, will not be fully free until all its citizens are free.

We preach freedom around the world, and we mean it, and we cherish our freedom here at home, but are we to say to the world, and much more importantly, to each other that this is the land of the free except for the Negroes; that we have no second-class citizens except Negroes; that we have no class or caste system, no ghettoes, no master race except with respect to Negroes?"

James Meredith, flanked by U.S. marshals, is escorted onto the University of Mississippi campus in 1962. When a riot broke out because racist whites believed blacks should not be able to attend school, two people were killed and some two hundred marshals and National Guardsmen were injured.

plained the situation to Americans in a radio and television address: "Mr. James Meredith is now in residence on the campus of the University of Mississippi. Our Nation is founded on the principle that observance of the law is the eternal safeguard of liberty and defiance of the law is the surest road to tyranny." [111]

But while the president was speaking, a riot broke out on campus. Demonstrators yelled "Go home, nigger!" [112] and threw rocks and Molotov cocktails at marshals, who responded with tear gas. Some two hundred Mississippi state troopers, who had been helping hold back an ugly crowd of some four thousand students and outsiders, had left a half-hour before the president spoke.

After his talk the president ordered the Mississippi National Guard onto the campus, but before peace was restored, a French reporter and a bystander were shot to death and some two hundred marshals and guardsmen were injured. U.S. marshals, obeying orders, never fired their guns.

The next day Meredith, accompanied by six marshals and a squad of soldiers, attended his first class; appropriately, it was on history, something he was making. Camped around Oxford, Mississippi, were three thousand soldiers. Meredith, who became the first African American graduate of "Ole Miss," was protected by armed marshals the entire time he attended the school.

1963—Civil Rights Explode

The civil rights fight came to a boil in April 1963 in Birmingham, Alabama, when King began a series of demonstrations and marches in what he called the most segregated city in America.

King and thousands of other African Americans, including schoolchildren, were arrested in marches and demonstrations. They were sprayed by fire hoses, beaten by police, attacked by police dogs, and taunted by racist, chanting crowds. And television brought the ugly scenes nightly to homes across America. Biographer Richard Reeves says television forced Kennedy to act more quickly than he desired:

> Kennedy preferred quiet negotiation. But that was impossible now in a televised America. Neither the president, nor the governor, nor the mayor, nor the police commissioner, nor the city's newspapers, nor the preachers had control any more of the flow of information coming from the streets and churches of that city. It was all on television—within hours, as film was developed and flown to New York or some other transmission center, then sent around the country on network cables and telephone lines. With those signals, the torch of communications was being passed to a new generation of technology, speeding up cycles of event-action-reaction-backlash, changing what people knew and when they knew it.[113]

Birmingham affected Kennedy deeply. When he saw a newspaper picture of a snarling dog lunging at a woman, he commented, "It makes me sick." He also said, "I can well understand why the Negroes of Birmingham are tired of being asked to be patient."[114]

Both Jack and Robert Kennedy worked behind the scenes to calm the situation, and influential local whites and African

Alabama governor George C. Wallace, a grim look of anger and defiance on his face, stands in the doorway of a building at the University of Alabama to block the admission of black students. President Kennedy used the power of his office to overcome Wallace's segregationist refusal to admit the students.

Americans eventually worked out their problems. But before peace was restored, two dynamite bombs exploded in Birmingham in front of the home of A. D. King, Martin's brother, and Kennedy again had to call out the National Guard to quell disorder.

Racial tensions had never been higher, and demonstrations continued throughout the South and spread to northern states. The Justice Department recorded 978 demonstrations in 209 cities from May 30 to August 8, 1963.

On June 10, after making his emotional plea for nuclear disarmament at American University, the president was told of another civil rights crisis—this time in Tuscaloosa, Alabama. Two African American students, Vivian Malone and James Hood, had enrolled in the University of Alabama and were to be admitted the next day. But Governor George Wallace—whose slogan was "Segregation now! Segregation tomorrow! Segregation Forever!"[115]—was poised to refuse them.

Kennedy ordered out the Alabama National Guard on June 11 to ensure Malone and Hood could enroll peacefully, which they did. For a second straight night the president addressed the nation to outline the historic civil rights bill he would soon propose. America, Kennedy said, was facing

> a moral crisis as a country and as a people. . . . Now the time has come for this Nation to fulfill its promise. The events in Birmingham and elsewhere have so increased the cries for equality that no city or State or legislative body can prudently choose to ignore them. The fires of frustration and discord are burning in every city, North and South, where legal remedies are not at hand.

> Redress is sought in the streets, in demonstrations, parades, and protests which create tensions and threaten violence and threaten lives.[116]

The president said he would propose legislation to end segregation in all public facilities such as hotels, restaurants, theaters, and retail stores. He also ordered the federal government to act more forcefully to end segregation and protect voting rights.

Kennedy had taken a stronger stand against racism than any other president. The president introduced a civil rights bill on June 22, but southern Democrats bottled it up in the Senate until after his death. It was passed in 1964.

The president's strong stand on this issue hurt him politically. He had more trouble getting legislation through Congress, and many Americans, who felt he was moving too fast, turned against him. Kennedy's approval rating in a November Gallup poll fell from 76 percent earlier in the year to 59 percent nationally and plummeted to 33 percent in the South.

"I Have a Dream"

The last big civil rights event of 1963 was the most joyous. On August 28, 1963, some four hundred thousand African Americans marched in Washington, D.C., to demonstrate their solidarity. Of all the moving words, the most memorable were from King.

> I still have a dream. It is a dream deeply rooted in the American dream. I have a dream that one day this nation

Rev. Martin Luther King Jr. delivers his "I have a dream" speech on August 28, 1963, a discourse that has been considered the most eloquent ever given on civil rights.

will rise up and live out the true meaning of its creed—we hold these truths to be self-evident, that all men are created equal—when we allow freedom to ring, when we let it ring from every village and hamlet, from every state and every city, we will be able to speed up that day when all of God's children—black men and white men, Jews and gentiles, Protestants and Catholics—will be able to join hands and sing in the words of the old Negro spiritual, "Free at last, free at last; thank God almighty, we are free at last."[117]

It was a dream that Kennedy now shared as well.

8 Dallas: A Fateful Day in History

Despite the many crises and problems John F. Kennedy endured during his presidency, one thing was clear—he had finally found a job he loved. In his biography *Kennedy,* Theodore Sorensen remarks that

> John F. Kennedy was a happy president. Happiness, he often said, is the full use of one's faculties along lines of excellence, and to him the presidency offered the ideal opportunity to pursue excellence. He liked the job, he thrived on its pressures. Disappointments only made him more determined. Only once do I recall his speaking with any bitterness about his post. It was a few minutes before he was to go on the air with the Cuban missile speech, and the Congressional leaders whom he called in for a briefing had presented a thousand objections and no new suggestions. More weary from their wranglings than his own week of deliberations, he remarked to me in disgust as he changed clothes for TV, "If they want this . . . job, they can have it." But moments later he was once again full of determination and drive; and at all times he made clear his pride of office.[118]

A Happier, Healthier JFK

In the fall of 1963 Kennedy was happier and healthier than at any time in his adult life. His Addison's disease and allergies were under control and his back, despite still being painful at times, was stronger than ever because he was swimming and following a strict exercise regiment. Kennedy looked fit, too, appearing strong and vigorous.

Kennedy had children late in life—Caroline was born in 1957, when he was forty, and John Jr. just a few weeks after he was elected president—but he joyously embraced fatherhood. And although the demands on a president are tremendous, it was easy for Kennedy to spend time with them because he worked at home in the White House. Caroline and John would often wander into meetings and climb up on his lap; sometimes they would just peek into the Oval Office to say hello.

According to *Triumph and Tragedy,* edited by Sidney C. Moody Jr.,

> The full measure of John Kennedy's love was directed toward his children, Caroline and John Jr. He was a devoted

President Kennedy was a loving father. Here he claps as his daughter, Caroline, and son, John Jr., dance in the Oval Office in 1962. Kennedy often took time from his duties to see his children.

father, but he really did not get to know his daughter until they moved into the White House . . . [where] Caroline and young John became national personalities; members of the press corps took every opportunity to photograph and question them. One day Caroline wandered into the press lobby and said her father was "sitting upstairs with his shoes and socks off not doing anything." Such quotable tidbits were grist for a public hungry about the first children to inhabit the White House in years. Like every devoted father, the President spent as much time with his children as possible.[119]

The president's personal life, however, was marred by two tragedies. The first occurred on December 19, 1961, when his father had a stroke that left him an invalid. This man who had commanded so much

power spent the rest of his life in a wheelchair, unable to speak. (He died November 19, 1969.)

The first time he visited his son in the Oval Office following his stroke, the president moved his father's wheelchair over to the rocking chair he used himself because of his bad back. He said softly: "This is my rocker, Dad. It looks as though we both need special chairs, doesn't it?"[120]

The second tragedy occurred on August 7, 1963, when his second son, Patrick Bouvier Kennedy, was born six weeks prematurely. The five-pound baby had trouble breathing and was critically ill; he died thirty-nine hours and twelve minutes after he was born. For the Kennedys, it was a tragedy made worse by the fact that Jackie had a miscarriage in 1953 and a stillbirth in 1956.

Kennedy had once said, "It is against the law of nature for parents to bury their children."[121] Now he had to bury his own son, and the death deeply affected him. Cardinal Richard Cushing, who presided over the funeral, said, "He wouldn't take his hands off that little coffin. I was afraid he'd carry it right out with him."[122]

The President and First Lady

The Kennedy marriage, rocky at times because of his unfaithfulness, also seemed to improve. In his years as president he had come to appreciate Jackie more as a person, partly because she had become a political star in her own right. The death of Patrick also drew them closer together.

At a party for their tenth anniversary on September 12, a change in their relationship was visible. "This was the first time," says *Washington Post* editor Benjamin Bradlee, "we had seen Jackie since the death of little Patrick. And she greeted JFK with by far the most affectionate embrace we had ever seen them give each other."[123] And Deputy Defense Secretary Roswell Gilpatrick later said, "There was a growing tenderness between them. I think their marriage was really beginning to work at the end."[124]

Kennedy, however, had hurt his wife by seeing other women. He continued this behavior as president, even having women come to the White House. Jackie

---

The President's Back

On May 16, shortly before leaving for Vienna and his first meeting with Nikita Khrushchev, President Kennedy severely injured his back in Ottawa, Canada, when he attended a ceremonial tree planting. He shoveled dirt several times and immediately injured his back. A new doctor in the White House then recommended exercise to strengthen the back. Peter Collier and David Horowitz write in The Kennedys *that after he began the exercises his back improved dramatically.*

"Yet he was in better shape than ever before. The steroids [cortisone] he had been taking had filled out his face so much that he fretted about having a weight problem, but the medication seemed to have controlled his Addison's disease for good. His back too had improved after his former doctor, Janet Travell, was replaced by White House physician George Bulkey. Bulkey had brought in a team of orthopedists who substituted a demanding regimen of exercises for the procaine injections [a local anesthetic that helped ease his back pain]. By the fall [of 1963] these exercises had succeeded so well, according to Bulkey, that Jack was able to go through 'a series of exercises which would do credit to a gymnast and was very pleased with his progress.'"

---

undoubtedly knew about some of his illicit relationships, but the general public never learned anything about his transgressions. In the years after his death, published reports linked him to movie stars like Marilyn Monroe and a woman named Judith Campbell, who was also the mistress of organized crime figure Sam Giancana. Kennedy severed that relationship in February 1962, after FBI director J. Edgar Hoover warned him about Campbell's ties to Giancana.

Stories about Kennedy's sexual misbehavior went unreported when he was alive because the media at that time believed that what public officials did in their private lives should be kept private. One biographer, Thomas C. Reeves, explains this attitude:

The largely all-male press corps at the time permitted certain misconduct by major public officials to go unreported. Drinking, womanizing, and homo-

Joseph P. Kennedy

The relationship between John F. Kennedy and his father was deep and complex. Critics often complained that the senior Kennedy "bought" elections for his son and unduly influenced him. But over the years Kennedy drew away from his father and became his own man. Kennedy biographers Herbert S. Parmet, in JFK: The Presidency of John F. Kennedy, *and Thomas C. Reeves, in* A Question of Character, *offer slightly different perspectives on the relationship at the time of the older man's stroke.*

PARMET: "Long before the illness the Ambassador's previous backstage presence had been minimized. He had become less prominent in the daily lives of his two oldest surviving sons. Acquaintances noted that he was less a part of their daily conversations. They loved, admired, and respected him. Nevertheless the reality was that their relationship had changed. The shy, bookish, introspective second son had grown up, had overcome the force of his own nature and met the paternal demands. He had become the leader."

REEVES: "Jack was not his father's puppet. Still, it is impossible to accept the contentions of family partisans that the ambassador rarely if ever gave Jack advice. . . . Bobby later recalled that after his father's debilitating illness, Jack 'often said how much he wished my father was well. On the tax bill and other matters that he would ordinarily talk to my father about, he could not do that any longer.' During the Cuban Missile Crisis, Rose burst into tears and said, 'My son, my poor, poor son, so much to bear and there is no way now for his father to help him.'"

A Campaign Trip to Dallas

President Kennedy, Jacqueline, Caroline, and John Jr. while on vacation at Hyannis Port, Massachusetts. This happy family portrait makes his assassination in Dallas all the more tragic.

Although elected by the narrowest of margins, Kennedy became a very popular president, and his poll ratings quickly shot up to 70 percent. Even the Bay of Pigs disaster did not make Americans lose faith in him. Several months after the failed invasion a Gallup poll showed his approval rating had jumped 10 points to 83 percent. "It's just like Eisenhower," he joked. "The worse I do, the more popular I get."[126]

Once elected, the public simply fell in love with the new president and his family. This is how the Kennedy biography *Triumph and Tragedy* explains the phenomenon:

> Why? Americans, one close associate of John Kennedy observed, "had confidence in him. They liked what he said and they liked his courage. But most of all they were young again." There were swing sets in the White House Rose Garden; Caroline's pony, named Macaroni, grazed on the White House lawn. Laughter, gay and young, echoed in the White House nursery, music and song in the White House drawing rooms.[127]

After two quiet terms under a conservative Republican administration, years often referred to as "the Boring Fifties," the new president's youthful energy and zest for life were a tonic for Americans. He made people feel stronger and more optimistic about the future.

Kennedy also boosted his popularity through his skillful use of the news media, especially frequent television news conferences. As biographer David Burner writes: "That his popularity rating never fell below 59 percent during his presidency was

sexuality were on the list unless these activities became unusually blatant or could be shown to affect the officeholder's public duties in a direct and pronounced way. Kennedy's sexual adventures, then, were off-limits to reporters in 1960 and Jack would enjoy that immunity for the rest of his life. In early 1963 a *New York Times* reporter told his editor that he had observed a prominent actress repeatedly visiting President Kennedy's New York hotel suite. "No story there," said the editor, and the matter was dropped.[125]

In President Kennedy, *Richard Reeves argues that John F. Kennedy was helped immeasurably by the sophisticated way he used the medium of television, which at the time was only just beginning to realize its potential.*

"The coming together of President and television was a new kind of American politics. 'We couldn't do it without TV,' Kennedy told [Press Secretary Pierre] Salinger. But neither of them knew what that meant. He had come to office at the end of politics' industrial age. The dominant visual medium as he began the 1960 campaign was black and white photography, people could rarely move faster than two hundred miles per hour on propeller driven airliners. But Kennedy had sensed a new politics as a farmer might feel a coming change in the weather. The great newspaper reader, the politician who seemed to hear the cocking of a camera at a hundred yards, was gripped by the fact that he could reach millions of Americans without first offering himself to the machines controlled by [the media]. This was a political miracle."

largely due to the press conferences, which almost every American witnessed at one time or another."[128]

But in the November 1963 Gallup poll his approval rating had fallen from 76 percent earlier in the year to 59 percent, a drop due almost entirely to negative reactions that arose over his strong stand on civil rights. Kennedy, facing a tough reelection campaign in 1964, was already courting voters.

That was why he went to Dallas, Texas, in November 1963.

A Premonition of Death?

Although it was the home state of Vice President Lyndon B. Johnson, in 1963 many Texas residents were hostile to Kennedy;

conservatives felt he was soft on communism and many, even those who were not bigoted, disapproved of his clarion call for racial equality.

The president visited three cities on Thursday, November 21, finishing with a speech in Fort Worth, where he spent the night. The next morning, before leaving for Dallas, Kennedy was reading a newspaper when he saw a large anti-Kennedy advertisement. "We're really heading into nut country today,"[129] Kennedy joked.

Many of his advisers had cautioned him not to make the trip to an area where many opposed him. His quip may have been sparked by his own concerns about Texas. That morning the president also made another comment, one which painfully foreshadowed his own death a few hours later.

Ill since childhood, Kennedy had lived his entire life knowing he could die unexpectedly. His own mortality was something he often discussed casually with friends, including his belief that a president was an easy target for an assassin. The president told aides who were traveling with him:

Last night would have been a hell of a night to assassinate a president. I mean it. There was the rain, and the night, and we were all getting jostled. Suppose a man had a pistol in a briefcase and he could have dropped the gun and the briefcase, and melted away in the crowd. If someone wanted to shoot me from a window with a rifle, nobody can stop it.[130]

Assassination

Air Force One touched down at Dallas's Love Field at 11:37 A.M. The president and his wife were greeted by cheers from people waving U.S. flags and carrying signs that said "Welcome Jack and Jackie to Big D." There were also a few anti-Kennedy protesters.

At 11:50 A.M. the president began the short ride to the Dallas Trade Mart to deliver a speech. Because it was a nice day, the plastic bubble top was removed from the presidential limousine, and its bulletproof side windows were rolled down so the crowd could have a better view of the president. Kennedy and Jackie sat in the backseat while Texas governor John Connally and his wife, Nellie, rode in front. They waved to the thousands of people who lined the streets to watch the motorcade.

As the presidential limousine was making a sharp left turn in Dealey Plaza past the seven-story-tall Texas School Book Depository, Mrs. Connally turned to the president and said, "You can't say that Dallas isn't friendly to you today."[131] The president's reply was cut short by the crack of the first of the bullets that would take his life. They seemed to come from the depository.

One bullet struck Kennedy in the throat, causing him to slump forward. Connally was also wounded by a bullet that went through his back, came out his chest, and lodged in his thigh. Another shot went wide and hit the roadway. Yet another shot exploded the right side of the president's head, throwing him violently to the left and then backward toward his wife.

"My God, what are they doing," Jackie screamed. "My God, they've killed Jack, they've killed my husband." She cradled her husband in her lap. "He's dead— they've killed him—oh, Jack, oh, Jack. I love you."[132]

The fourth assassination of a U.S. president occurred at 12:30 P.M. It had taken less than six seconds.

Secret service agents leaped out of cars behind the presidential limousine, weapons drawn, but there was no one to shoot at. The motorcade then sped to Parkland Hospital, where the Reverends Oscar Huber and James Thompson gave Kennedy the last rites. The president was declared dead at 1 P.M.

The nation was in a perilous situation without a leader, but the vice president had been in the motorcade. Immediately after Kennedy was declared dead, Johnson was rushed to the airport so he could return to Washington.

Less than three hours after the shots were fired, Johnson was sworn in as the

The Texas School Book Depository, the warehouse from which Lee Harvey Oswald fired the shots that killed President Kennedy. A witness told officials investigating the assassination that from his vantage point in window A he could see a man with a rifle fire shots from window B, which was directly below him.

nation's thirty-sixth president aboard Air Force One. He took the oath flanked by his wife, Lady Bird, and Jackie Kennedy. The First Lady had refused to change her pink wool suit, whose skirt bore her husband's blood stains. "It's his blood," she said. "I do not want to remove this. I want them to see what they have done." [133]

Lee Harvey Oswald

At 12:45 P.M. police radios broadcast a description of an employee missing from the book depository. At 1:15 P.M. patrolman J. D. Tippit saw a man that fit the description of the worker about two miles from Dealey Plaza. When he stopped his squad car to question the man, Tippit was shot three times with a .38 caliber revolver and died instantly.

Witnesses helped police track down the suspect in the Tippit shooting to the Texas Theater. Police entered the movie theater at 1:45 P.M. and arrested a man who drew a .38 caliber revolver and shouted, "This is it!" [134] His gun misfired and no one was hurt.

The suspect was twenty-four-year-old Lee Harvey Oswald, the man police believed killed both the president and Tippit. His fingerprints were found on the rifle that ballistic tests proved was the one that had been fired from the sixth floor of the depository. There was also proof that Oswald had purchased the 6.5 millimeter carbine and was in the building when the president was killed.

Oswald had served three years in the U.S. Marines. After a dishonorable discharge in 1959, Oswald, who was a communist sympathizer, defected to Moscow. Oswald, however, returned to the United

States in 1962 with his Russian-born wife, Marina, and the couple settled in the Dallas–Fort Worth area.

On Saturday Oswald was charged with murder. On Sunday morning, while being transferred to a county facility, a man named Jack Ruby shot Oswald to death in the basement of the city jail. Owner of a local nightclub, Ruby had been allowed into the high-security area because he was known by a number of Dallas police officers.

As he shot Oswald, Ruby shouted, "You killed my president, you rat!"[135] Tens of millions of Americans were horrified as they witnessed the murder live on television.

The facts in the aftermath of the assassination are simple. But the events were so bizarre, happened so quickly, and left so many questions unanswered that many people wondered whether the public had been told the whole truth about the slaying of President Kennedy. Did Oswald act alone, or were there others involved in a conspiracy to kill the president? Had Ruby been ordered to kill Oswald to prevent the full story from ever being revealed?

In the years since 1963, many new details have emerged and countless conspiracy theories have been put forth about the death of the president. None has ever

Just hours after President Kennedy was assassinated, Vice President Lyndon B. Johnson takes the presidential oath of office aboard Air Force One. To his right is Jackie Kennedy and to his left his wife, Lady Bird Johnson. The pink wool suit Jackie wore was stained with the blood of her husband.

been proven. Thus, the conclusion of the Warren Commission, the investigative panel appointed by President Johnson, remains the final official verdict. Published in October 1964, the report states that Oswald acted alone and killed both the president and Tippit: "Based upon the investigation reviewed in this chapter, the Commission concluded that there is no credible evidence that Lee Harvey Oswald was part of a conspiracy to assassinate President Kennedy. Examination of the facts . . . revealed no indication that Oswald was aided in the planning or execution of his scheme."[136]

Dallas nightclub owner Jack Ruby steps forward and shoots Lee Harvey Oswald while Oswald is being transferred from the city jail to another facility.

A snapshot of Lee Harvey Oswald, the former U.S. Marine who killed President Kennedy. He is holding a rifle and a pro-communist newspaper.

Kennedy was the fourth president in U.S. history to be shot to death. The others were Abraham Lincoln, James Garfield, and William McKinley.

A Hero's Farewell

At 12:34 P.M. a United Press International (UPI) bulletin flashed across the nation's news wires: "Three shots were fired at President Kennedy's motorcade today in down-

The Undelivered Dallas Speech

Kennedy had planned to deliver a speech at the Trade Mart in Dallas the day of his assassination. The speech was going to address the problems facing America and the steps the president proposed to correct them. This is how it would have concluded.

"I cite these facts and figures to make it clear that America today is stronger than ever before. Our adversaries have not abandoned their ambitions, our dangers have not diminished, our vigilance cannot be relaxed. But now we have the military, the scientific, and the economic strength to do whatever must be done for the preservation and promotion of freedom.

That strength will never be used in pursuit of aggressive ambitions—it will always be used in pursuit of peace. It will never be used to promote provocations—it will always be used to promote the peaceful settlement of disputes.

We in this country, in this generation, are—by destiny rather than choice—the watchmen on the walls of world freedom. We ask, therefore, that we may be worthy of our power and responsibility, that we may exercise our strength with wisdom and restraint, and that we may achieve in our time and for all time the ancient vision of 'peace on earth, good will toward men.' That must always be our goal, and the righteousness of our cause must always underlie our strength. For as was written long ago: 'except the Lord keep the city, the watchman waketh but in vain.'"

town Dallas."[137] UPI's urgent report from Dealey Plaza was the first on the assassination. Within a half hour the media began informing the world the president indeed had been killed.

For all of that day and through Kennedy's funeral in Washington on Monday, Americans were able to watch history being made. Television, an infant medium still trying to fulfill its vast potential, became the eyes and ears of the nation and millions sat glued to their sets. They saw news anchor Walter Cronkite fight back tears as he reported Kennedy's death and then stay on air for hours, channeling bits and pieces of information as they became available.

A grieving nation watched the coffin bearing the president's body being unloaded in Washington; witnessed Ruby gun down Oswald; saw a quarter of a million people file by the president's bier in the Capitol Rotunda; and experienced the

As the flag-draped coffin bearing President Kennedy's body passes by, John F. Kennedy Jr. (far right) delivers an affectionate, final salute to his slain father. This touching scene, transmitted live on television and recreated the next day in newspapers around the world, captured the heartbreaking reality of Kennedy's death.

solemn dignity of the funeral of a world leader. It was one of the most emotional weeks in the nation's history.

Americans mourned not only for Kennedy but also for his family. They watched in awe as Jackie, elegantly calm throughout but her face etched with undeniable sadness, carried out her role as widow of the slain president with grace and dignity.

The most vivid scene of all, one etched forever in the minds of viewers, was of Jackie,

clad in widow's black, holding the hands of Caroline and John as their father's coffin left the White House one last time. The saddest was the timid little military salute John Jr. gave his father's casket as it left St. Matthew's Cathedral after the funeral mass November 25.

That Monday was also John's third birthday. It would forever be remembered as the day his father was laid to rest in Arlington National Cemetery.

The Darkness and the Light

John F. Kennedy liked to quote Abraham Lincoln: "There are few things wholly evil or wholly good. Almost everything, especially of Government policy, is an inseparable compound of the two, so that our best judgment of the preponderance between them is continually demanded." [138]

People are also a mix of good and bad. Kennedy's public policy was not without its faults and neither was his character. Kennedy is most often criticized for being too ambitious, for the calculating way he shaped his public image, and for his ruthless political maneuvering. Most politicians who have sought the presidency, however, have had the same weaknesses.

Theodore Sorensen believes what set Kennedy apart was his ability to learn, even from his mistakes. "If one extraordinary quality stood out among the many, it was the quality of continuing growth," he writes. "In November 1963 he had learned more about the uses and limitations of power, about the men on whom he could depend, about the adversaries and evils he faced, and about the tools and techniques of policy. " [139]

JFK's Legacy

Kennedy's biggest challenge was communism. He blundered badly over the Bay of Pigs, making the mistake of trusting the military "experts" who said the invasion would work. He never did again. During the Cuban missile crisis he surrounded himself with people he could trust and fully considered all the facts and options. The president then acted boldly to defuse the situation.

More importantly, when he sensed a shift in Soviet attitudes, Kennedy seized the opportunity to secure a nuclear test ban treaty. One of his greatest legacies, the treaty began an era of improving relations between the rival superpowers. The two bitter rivals never again came as close to war as they had in the fall of 1962.

During Kennedy's presidency Vietnam was a powder keg waiting to explode. It did, with disastrous results, under President Lyndon B. Johnson: Within a year of Kennedy's death, Johnson had increased the number of U.S. soldiers in Vietnam from 16,000 to 231,000.

No one knows what Kennedy would have done. But key aides said years later that shortly before his death the president told them he had decided to withdraw from Vietnam if he was reelected in 1964. "In 1965, I'll become one of the most unpopular presidents in history. I'll be damned everywhere as an appeaser. But I don't care. If I tried to pull out completely now from

Vietnam, we would have another Joe McCarthy red [communist] scare on our hands," Kennedy said, "but I can do it after I'm re-elected."[140]

Kennedy understood that the United States, like France, could not win a guerrilla war in the jungle against "an enemy which is everywhere and at the same time nowhere, an 'enemy of the people' which has the sympathy and covert support of the people."[141]

He also realized how quickly U.S. troop commitments could escalate once they began. "It will be just like Berlin," Kennedy said of a potential buildup in Vietnam. "The troops will march in; the band will play; the crowds will cheer; and in four days everyone will have forgotten. Then we will be told we have to send in more troops. It's like taking a drink. The effect wears off, and you have to take another."[142] That is exactly what happened in Vietnam under Johnson.

It would have taken great political courage to withdraw from Vietnam, the kind he had written about in *Profiles of Courage*. Many feel Kennedy would have shown that brand of courage on Vietnam, sparing the nation from a divisive war that damaged its international prestige and all but ruined its economy.

Just as Vietnam was unfinished business when Kennedy died, so were his civil rights bill and tax cut proposals. Both were approved under the Johnson administration, partly because of the tidal wave of

President Kennedy's assassination changed the course of U.S. history. Many believe that if Kennedy had lived and won reelection in 1964, the United States might not have become so heavily involved in the war in South Vietnam, a conflict that would divide the nation for decades to come.

love and admiration for Kennedy that developed after his death and partly because Johnson knew how to push the measures through Congress. The civil rights bill put the government squarely behind African Americans' struggle for equality, and the tax bill sent the economy soaring.

In 1969 the space program met Kennedy's lunar-landing timetable. President Dwight D. Eisenhower had never considered the space program a priority, but Kennedy, showing far greater vision for the future, realized its importance.

It was his ability to make Americans believe they could do anything and feel that the future, clouded so long by the threat of communism, racial unrest, and economic uncertainty, held a bright new promise that made Kennedy so effective and so beloved.

Camelot

After Kennedy died, his wife and friends tried to make the story of Camelot, which is about King Arthur, an allegory for Kennedy's tragically shortened presidency. Jackie first introduced the idea in an interview with journalist Theodore H. White.

I realized history made Jack what he was. You must think of him as this little boy, sick so much of the time, reading the Knights of the Round Table. For Jack, history was full of heroes. And if it made him this way—if it made him see the heroes—maybe other little boys will see. Men are such a combination of good and bad. Jack had this hero idea of history, the idealistic view . . . there'll never be another Camelot again.[143]

Thus started the final mythification of his life—Kennedy as King Arthur, fighting against evil. For a decade after his death, books written about Kennedy, especially by those close to him like Sorensen and Arthur M. Schlesinger Jr., cast Kennedy in saintlike terms. After that, authors began taking a more balanced look, with several anti-Kennedy writers dredging up every possible negative story about him in an attempt to destroy his reputation.

But even his critics admit Kennedy grew in office. *New York Times* writer James Reston said it best when he wrote of Kennedy's assassination: "What was killed was not only the President but the promise."[144]

A promise that would never be fulfilled.

Notes

Introduction: A Life of Triumph and Tragedy

1. Quoted in Richard Reeves, *President Kennedy: Profile of Power*. New York: Simon & Schuster, 1993, p. 19.

2. Quoted in John H. Davis, *The Kennedys: Dynasty and Disaster*. New York: McGraw-Hill, 1984, p. 113.

3. Quoted in Arthur M. Schlesinger Jr., *A Thousand Days: John F. Kennedy in the White House*. Boston: Houghton Mifflin, 1965, p. 4.

Chapter 1: Growing Up a Kennedy

4. James MacGregor Burns, *John Kennedy: A Political Profile*. New York: Harcourt, Brace & World, 1961, p. 6.

5. Quoted in Sidney C. Moody Jr., ed., *Triumph and Tragedy: The Story of the Kennedys*. New York: Associated Press, 1968, p. 7.

6. Quoted in Burns, *John Kennedy*, p. 20.

7. Quoted in Thomas C. Reeves, *A Question of Character: A Life of John F. Kennedy*. Rocklin, CA: Prima, 1992, p. 29.

8. Quoted in Burns, *John Kennedy*, p. 21.

9. Quoted in Herbert S. Parmet, *Jack: The Struggles of John F. Kennedy*. New York: Dial Press, 1980, p. 21.

10. Quoted in Zachary Kent, *Encyclopedia of Presidents, John F. Kennedy, Thirty-Fifth President of the United States*. Chicago: Childrens Press, 1987, p. 14.

11. Parmet, *Jack*, p. 45.

12. Reeves, *A Question of Character*, p. 39.

13. Quoted in Ralph G. Martin, *A Hero for Our Time: An Intimate Story of the Kennedy Years*. New York: Macmillan, 1983, p. 36.

14. Quoted in Reeves, *A Question of Character*, p. 44.

15. Quoted in William Manchester, *One Brief Shining Moment: Remembering Kennedy*. Boston: Little, Brown, 1983, p. 55.

Chapter 2: JFK: Author, War Hero

16. Quoted in Theodore Sorensen, *Kennedy*. New York: Harper & Row, 1965, p. 18.

17. John F. Kennedy, *Why England Slept*. New York: Wilfred Funk, 1961, p. 223.

18. Kennedy, *Why England Slept*, p. 230.

19. Quoted in David Burner, *John F. Kennedy and a New Generation*. Boston: Little, Brown, 1988, p. 13.

20. Quoted in Moody, *Triumph and Tragedy*, p. 70.

21. Quoted in Davis, *The Kennedys*, p. 120.

22. Parmet, *Jack*, p. 91.

23. Quoted in Martin S. Goldman, *John F. Kennedy: Portrait of a President*. New York: Facts On File, 1995, p. 19.

24. Quoted in Robert J. Donovan, *PT 109: John F. Kennedy in World War II*. Greenwich, CT: Fawcett, 1961, p. 103.

25. Quoted in Donovan, *PT 109*, p. 127.

26. Quoted in Kent, *Encyclopedia of Presidents*, p. 33.

27. Quoted in Burner, *John F. Kennedy and a New Generation*, p. 21.

28. Quoted in Kent, *Encyclopedia of Presidents*, p. 37.

29. Quoted in Martin, *A Hero for Our Time*, p. 48.

30. Schlesinger, *A Thousand Days*, p. 15.

Chapter 3: JFK Goes to Washington

31. Quoted in Goldman, *John F. Kennedy*, p. 33.

32. Quoted in Manchester, *One Brief Shining Moment*, p. 24.

33. Quoted in Moody, *Triumph and Tragedy*, p. 94.

34. Quoted in Goldman, *John F. Kennedy*, p. 32.

35. Quoted in Manchester, *One Brief Shining Moment*, p. 24.

36. Quoted in Burns, *John Kennedy*, p. 71.

37. Quoted in Moody, *Triumph and Tragedy*, p. 105.

38. Quoted in Manchester, *One Brief Shining Moment*, p. 58.

39. Quoted in Burns, *John Kennedy*, p. 80.

40. Quoted in Moody, *Triumph and Tragedy*, p. 107.

41. Burns, *John Kennedy*, p. 95.

42. Quoted in Burns, *John Kennedy*, p. 93.

43. Victor Lasky, *JFK: The Man and the Myth*. New York: Macmillan, 1963, p. 99.

44. Parmet, *Jack*, p. 167.

45. Moody, *Triumph and Tragedy*, p. 103.

46. Quoted in Parmet, *Jack*, p. 190.

47. Quoted in Reeves, *President Kennedy*, p. 24.

Chapter 4: Senator Kennedy: Success, Love, Pain

48. Quoted in Burns, *John Kennedy*, p. 93.

49. Quoted in Reeves, *A Question of Character*, p. 95.

50. Quoted in Peter Collier and David Horowitz, *The Kennedys: An American Drama*. New York: Simon & Schuster, 1984, p.185.

51. Burns, *John Kennedy*, p. 113.

52. Quoted in Kent, *Encyclopedia of Presidents*, p. 46.

53. Burns, *John Kennedy*, p. 116.

54. Quoted in Martin, *A Hero for Our Time*, p. 61.

55. Quoted in Burns, *John Kennedy*, p. 127.

56. Quoted in Moody, *Triumph and Tragedy*, p. 118.

57. Quoted in Parmet, *Jack*, p. 260.

58. Sorensen, *Kennedy*, p. 27.

59. Quoted in Sorensen, *Kennedy*, p. 59.

60. Quoted in Burns, *John Kennedy*, p. 197.

61. Quoted in Kent, *Encyclopedia of Presidents*, p. 53.

62. Quoted in Reeves, *A Question of Character*, p. 125.

63. Quoted in Moody, *Triumph and Tragedy*, p. 128.

64. Sorensen, *Kennedy*, p. 68.

65. Sorensen, *Kennedy*, p. 70.

66. Parmet, *Jack*, p. 333.

67. Quoted in Robert Kelley, *The Shaping of the American Past*, 4th ed., vol. 2. Englewood Cliffs, NJ: Prentice-Hall, 1986, p. 684.

68. Quoted in Goldman, *John F. Kennedy*, p. 54.

Chapter 5: JFK: The New Frontier

69. Quoted in Burns, *John Kennedy*, p. 217.

70. John F. Kennedy (speech given in Senate Caucus Room), January 20, 1960, John Fitzgerald Kennedy Library and Museum website. On-line. Internet. Available http://www.cs.umb.edu/jfklibrary/speeches/htm.

71. Quoted in Sorensen, *Kennedy*, p. 77.

72. Quoted in Manchester, *One Brief Shining Moment*, p. 93.

73. Quoted in Sorensen, *Kennedy*, p. 135.

74. Quoted in Theodore H. White, *The Making of the President, 1960*. New York: Atheneum, 1961, p. 108.

75. Quoted in Sorensen, *Kennedy*, p. 141.

76. John F. Kennedy (speech given at Democratic Convention in Los Angeles, California), July 15, 1960, John Fitzgerald Kennedy Library and Museum website. On-line. Internet. Available http://www.cs.umb.edu/jfklibrary/speeches/htm.

77. Quoted in Collier and Horowitz, *The Kennedys*, p. 244.

78. Quoted in Lasky, *JFK*, p. 474.

79. Quoted in White, *The Making of the President, 1960,* p. 323.

80. John F. Kennedy (inaugural speech), January 20, 1961, John Fitzgerald Kennedy Library and Museum website. On-line. Internet. Available http://www.cs.umb.edu/jfklibrary/speeches/htm.

81. Quoted in Moody, *Triumph and Tragedy,* p. 163.

82. Quoted in Goldman, *John F. Kennedy,* p. 85.

Chapter 6: JFK and the Challenge of Communism

83. Quoted in Sorensen, *Kennedy,* p. 511.

84. Quoted in Reeves, *President Kennedy,* p. 37.

85. Quoted in Manchester, *One Brief Shining Moment,* p. 188.

86. John F. Kennedy (speech given to Congress), July 25, 1961, John Fitzgerald Kennedy Library and Museum website. On-line. Internet. Available http://www.cs.umb.edu/jfklibrary/speeches/htm.

87. Quoted in Burner, *John F. Kennedy and a New Generation,* p. 4.

88. Quoted in Herbert S. Parmet, *JFK: The Presidency of John F. Kennedy.* New York: Dial Press, 1983, p. 98.

89. Quoted in Sorensen, *Kennedy,* p. 530.

90. Quoted in Martin, *A Hero for Our Time,* p. 460.

91. John F. Kennedy (speech given on national television), October 22, 1962, John Fitzgerald Kennedy Library and Museum website. On-line. Internet. Available http://www.cs.umb.edu/jfklibrary/speeches/htm.

92. John F. Kennedy (speech given on national television), October 22, 1962, John Fitzgerald Kennedy Library and Museum website. On-line. Internet. Available http://www.cs.umb.edu/jfklibrary/speeches/htm.

93. Quoted in Barbara Harrison and Daniel Terris, *A Twilight Struggle: The Life of John Fitzgerald Kennedy.* New York: Lothrop, Lee & Shepard Books, 1992, p. 118.

94. Quoted in Parmet, *JFK,* p. 310.

95. John F. Kennedy (speech given to graduating students at American University, Washington, D.C.), June 10, 1963, John Fitzgerald Kennedy Library and Museum website. On-line. Internet. Available http://www.cs.umb.edu/jfklibrary/ speeches/htm.

96. John F. Kennedy, John Fitzgerald Kennedy Library and Museum website. On-line. Internet. Available http://www.cs.umb.edu/jfklibrary.

97. John F. Kennedy (speech given in Rudolph Wilde Platz, West Berlin), June 26, 1963, John Fitzgerald Library and Museum website. On-line. Internet. Available http://www.cs.umb.edu/jfklibrary/speeches/htm.

98. Quoted in Samuel Eliot Morison, *The Oxford History of the American People.* New York: Penguin Books, 1994, p. 496.

99. Quoted in Manchester, *One Brief Shining Moment,* p. 216.

100. Quoted in Goldman, *John F. Kennedy,* p. 127.

101. Quoted in George McTurnan Kahin and John Wilson Lewis, *The United States in Vietnam.* New York: Dial Press, 1967, p. 144.

Chapter 7: Other Challenges: Civil Rights, Space, the Economy

102. Quoted in Burns, *John Kennedy,* p. 155.

103. Burner, *John F. Kennedy and a New Generation,* p. 36.

104. Quoted in Reeves, *President Kennedy,* p. 275.

105. Quoted in Reeves, *President Kennedy,* p. 452.

106. John F. Kennedy (speech given to Congress), May 25, 1961, John Fitzgerald Kennedy Library and Museum website. On-line. Internet. Available http://www.cs.umb.edu/jfklibrary/speeches.htm.

107. John F. Kennedy (speech given to Congress), May 25, 1961, John Fitzgerald Kennedy

Library and Museum website. On-line. Internet. Available http://www.cs.umb.edu/jfklibrary/speeches.htm.

108. Quoted in Reeves, *President Kennedy*, p. 464.

109. Quoted in Schlesinger, *A Thousand Days*, p. 957.

110. Quoted in Robert Kelley, *The Shaping of the American Past*, vol. 2, p. 700.

111. John F. Kennedy (speech given on national television), September 30, 1962, John Fitzgerald Kennedy Library and Museum website. On-line. Internet. Available http://www.cs.umb.edu/jfklibrary/ speeches.htm.

112. Quoted in Goldman, *John F. Kennedy*, p. 97.

113. Quoted in Reeves, *President Kennedy*, p. 488.

114. Quoted in Manchester, *One Brief Shining Moment*, p. 237.

115. Quoted in Martin, *A Hero for Our Time*, p. 512.

116. John F. Kennedy (speech given on national television), June 11, 1963, John Fitzgerald Kennedy Library and Museum website. On-line. Internet. Available http://www.cs.umb.edu/jfklibrary/speeches.htm.

117. Quoted in Goldman, *John F. Kennedy*, p. 103.

Chapter 8: Dallas: A Fateful Day in History

118. Sorensen, *Kennedy*, p. 366.

119. Moody, *Triumph and Tragedy*, p. 166.

120. Quoted in Martin, *A Hero for Our Time*, p. 436.

121. Quoted in Moody, *Triumph and Tragedy*, p. 184.

122. Quoted in Moody, *Triumph and Tragedy*, p. 185.

123. Quoted in Parmet, *JFK*, p. 337.

124. Quoted in Reeves, *A Question of Character*, p. 401.

125. Reeves, *A Question of Character*, pp. 202–203.

126. Quoted in Manchester, *One Brief Shining Moment*, p. 137.

127. Moody, *Triumph and* Tragedy, p. 165.

128. Burner, *John F. Kennedy and a New Generation*, p. 60.

129. Quoted in Edward Klein, *All Too Human: The Love Story of Jack and Jackie Kennedy*. New York: Pocket Books, 1996, p. 343.

130. Quoted in Klein, *All Too Human*, p. 343.

131. Quoted in United Press International and *American Heritage* Magazine, *Four Days: The Historical Record of the Death of President Kennedy*. New York: American Heritage, 1964, p. 14.

132. Quoted in Harrison and Terris, *A Twilight Struggle*, p. 4.

133. Quoted in Martin, *A Hero for Our Time*, p. 558.

134. Quoted in United Press International and *American Heritage* Magazine, *Four Days*, p. 31.

135. Quoted in David Pietrusza, *John F. Kennedy*. San Diego: Lucent Books, 1997, p. 38.

136. *The Official Warren Commission Report on the Assassination of President John F. Kennedy*. Garden City, NY: Doubleday, 1964, p. 374.

137. United Press International and *American Heritage* Magazine, *Four Days*, p. 22.

Epilogue: The Darkness and the Light

138. Quoted in Schlesinger, *A Thousand Days*, p. 110.

139. Sorensen, *Kennedy*, p. 752.

140. Quoted in Kenneth P. O'Donnell and David Powers, with Joe McCarthy, *"Johnny We Hardly Knew Ye": Memories of John Fitzgerald Kennedy*. Boston: Little, Brown, 1970, p. 16.

141. Quoted in Goldman, *John F. Kennedy*, p. 125.

142. Quoted in Burner, *John F. Kennedy and a New Generation*, p. 100.

143. Quoted in Manchester, *One Brief Shining Moment*, p. 273.

144. Quoted in Martin, *A Hero for Our Time*, p. 568.

For Further Reading

Bill Adler, ed., *The Kennedy Wit.* New York: Citadel Press, 1964. This short, humorous volume provides examples of the humor that was so much a part of the Kennedy charm. Entertaining while at the same time illuminating that part of his personality.

Robert J. Donovan, *PT 109: John F. Kennedy in World War II.* Greenwich, CT: Fawcett, 1961. The major source of information for the World War II experiences of Kennedy. The author visited the scene of the action in the Solomon Islands and interviewed Kennedy, surviving members of PT 109, and other people who were involved.

Barbara Harrison and Daniel Terris, *A Twilight Struggle: The Life of John Fitzgerald Kennedy.* New York: Lothrop, Lee & Shepard Books, 1992. A basic telling of the life of Kennedy. It explains issues in an easy-to-read manner without going into great detail or complexity.

John F. Kennedy, *Profiles in Courage.* New York: Harper & Brothers, 1956. This Pulitzer Prize–winning book takes an interesting look at the role political courage played in the lives of a handful of U.S. politicians Kennedy admired. Personal courage was a trait Kennedy valued deeply and believed played a major role in shaping many important events in U.S. history.

Zachary Kent, *Encyclopedia of Presidents, John F. Kennedy: Thirty-Fifth President of the United States.* Chicago: Childrens Press, 1987. A straightforward account of the life of John F. Kennedy. An easy-to-understand biography of one of the nation's most intriguing presidents.

Sidney C. Moody Jr., ed., *Triumph and Tragedy: The Story of the Kennedys.* New York: Associated Press, 1968. Written by reporters and editors of the Associated Press wire service, this book is a readable account of the president's life. However, it fails to give any really penetrating insights into Kennedy, either as a man or a political figure. It also retains the almost worshiping view of Kennedy that existed for several years after his death. It includes many excellent photographs.

Kenneth P. O'Donnell and David Powers, with Joe McCarthy, *"Johnny We Hardly Knew Ye": Memories of John Fitzgerald Kennedy.* Boston: Little, Brown, 1970. This book by O'Donnell and Powers, friends and confidants of their subject for fifteen years, is an interesting personal look at Kennedy. Its main strength is the intimate look they give into Kennedy's life.

David Pietrusza, *John F. Kennedy.* San Diego: Lucent Books, 1997. Facts that have emerged since Kennedy's assassination have spawned a variety of conspiracy theories. This book reviews the major theories and is an interesting look at the confusing, emotional aftermath of his death.

United Press International and *American Heritage* Magazine, *Four Days: The*

Historical Record of the Death of President Kennedy. New York: American Heritage, 1964. This book is based on stories written by reporters and editors of the United Press International wire service after Kennedy's assassination. Easy-to-read and illustrated with great pictures that help the reader understand the emotions of this difficult period in U.S. history.

Works Consulted

David Burner, *John F. Kennedy and a New Generation.* Boston: Little, Brown, 1988. A balanced look at the life of Kennedy that does not ignore his flaws. It gives the reader a thorough understanding of his personality and his effect on the events of his time.

James MacGregor Burns, *John Kennedy: A Political Profile.* New York: Harcourt, Brace & World, 1961. Written in cooperation with Kennedy before the 1960 presidential election, this biography is one of the seminal works on his early life. Although biased at times toward Kennedy, this work has become a major information source for later biographies.

Peter Collier and David Horowitz, *The Kennedys: An American Drama.* New York: Simon & Schuster, 1984. An in-depth study of the Kennedy family from the time the president's ancestors immigrated to America through the problems experienced by the children of John, Robert, and Edward in the early 1980s. It reports the many tragedies that have befallen this family, many of their own making.

John H. Davis, *The Kennedys: Dynasty and Disaster.* New York: McGraw-Hill, 1984. An in-depth look at the Kennedy family, from founding father Joseph through the children of President Kennedy and his brothers and sisters. It examines how being a Kennedy affected all of them through the generations.

Martin S. Goldman, *John F. Kennedy: Portrait of a President.* New York: Facts On File, 1995. A solid biography that outlines the life of Kennedy and uses many sources to tell his story. Goldman is balanced in the way he considers the president's personality and his role in history.

George McTurnan Kahin and John Wilson Lewis, *The United States in Vietnam.* New York: Dial Press, 1967. The Vietnam War was an important conflict in the nation's history. The authors examine how the United States became involved in this decisive war.

Robert Kelly, *The Shaping of the American Past.* 4th ed., vol. 2. Englewood Cliffs, NJ: Prentice-Hall, 1986. This book examines the way America's history was shaped by both historical events and the people involved. It is an insightful history of the United States.

John Fitzgerald Kennedy Library and Museum website. On-line. Internet. Available http://www.cs.umb.edu/jfklibrary. The official Internet website for the John Fitzgerald Kennedy Library and Museum is a wonderful place to go for more information on JFK's life. It contains original documents of his speeches, detailed biographical information, sound and video, plus links to other sites.

John F. Kennedy, *Why England Slept.* New York: Wilfred Funk, 1961. Kennedy's examination of why it took England so long to respond to the challenge from Germany.

Edward Klein, *All Too Human: The Love Story of Jack and Jackie Kennedy.* New York:

Pocket Books, 1996. A journalist who knew Jackie Kennedy reports on their relationship from the time Kennedy courted her through his death. A personality piece and not a historical work.

Victor Lasky, *JFK: The Man and the Myth*. New York: Macmillan, 1963. Written before Kennedy's assassination, it is the first work highly critical of Kennedy. The book describes in detail the political maneuvering of Kennedy, his father, and brother Robert to get what they wanted—the presidency.

William Manchester, *Remembering Kennedy: One Brief Shining Moment*. Boston: Little Brown, 1983. Manchester, a history professor and author who first met Kennedy in 1946, provides a glowing tribute to Kennedy's life. It glosses over his failings but is well written and captures the feel of Kennedy's personality and provides valuable insights into his psychological makeup.

Ralph G. Martin, *A Hero for Our Time: An Intimate Story of the Kennedy Years*. New York: Macmillan, 1983. A very readable biography of Kennedy. It concentrates on Kennedy's personal life, providing a good image of Kennedy the man. However, it does not cover in detail the complexities of the issues he had to deal with as president.

Samuel Eliot Morison, *The Oxford History of the American People*. New York: Penguin Books, 1994. One of the nation's most respected historians provides information and comments on the history of the United States. His insights will help readers understand why certain events happened and how they affected the nation.

The Official Warren Commission Report on the Assassination of President John F. Kennedy. Garden City, NY: Doubleday, 1964. The lengthy, complex Warren Commission report exhaustively examines every detail in the assassination of the president. This publication includes pictures that help make the report come alive for the reader as well as historical commentary by Bruce Catton and analysis by legal expert Louis Nizer.

Herbert S. Parmet, *Jack: The Struggles of John F. Kennedy*. New York: Dial Press, 1980. The first of two volumes on Kennedy is a thorough look at his life. It unmasks some of the myths surrounding Kennedy and treats him objectively.

————, *JFK: The Presidency of John F. Kennedy*. New York: Dial Press, 1983. The second volume, a meticulous study of Kennedy's brief presidency, provides a detailed, balanced look at how he functioned as chief executive. It is filled with inside details of how decisions were made and the emotions Kennedy and other participants had during the Cuban missile crisis and other major events.

Richard Reeves, *President Kennedy: Profile of Power*. New York: Simon & Schuster, 1993. An exhaustive, almost day-by-day account of Kennedy's presidency. Reeves had access to documents released long after Kennedy's death that shed new light on the decisions he made as president. Perhaps the best study of Kennedy as president ever written.

Thomas C. Reeves, *A Question of Character: A Life of John F. Kennedy*. Rocklin, CA:

Prima, 1992. Just about every negative quote and story about Kennedy shows up in this book. It destroys some of the myths surrounding Kennedy and provides valuable insights into his darker side, but it is so unbalanced that at times the reader may question the author's believability.

Arthur M. Schlesinger Jr., *A Thousand Days: John F. Kennedy in the White House*. Boston: Houghton Mifflin, 1965. This personal memoir of Kennedy's presidency by one of his top aides won a Pulitzer Prize for biography. Despite providing fine details of the events and some insights into Kennedy's personality, it generally puts a positive spin on every event while ignoring Kennedy's flaws and the mistakes he made.

Theodore Sorensen, *Kennedy*. New York: Harper & Row, 1965. This well-written biography, by the man considered for many years to be Kennedy's alter ego, articulates Kennedy's personality as few other books ever have. But like Schlesinger, Sorensen lacks balance and at times is worshipful of his subject.

Theodore H. White, *The Making of the President, 1960*. New York: Atheneum, 1961. The finest book to date about a presidential election, it provides valuable detail and insight into how Kennedy became president. Although campaigning and politics have changed in many ways since then, it is a valuable resource in understanding presidential politics.

Index

Adams, John Quincy, 48
Addison's disease, 12, 22,
    39–40, 46, 91, 93
Africa, 68
African Americans
    on Kennedy's senatorial
        staff, 46
    march on Washington, D.C.,
        89–90
    report of U.S. Civil Rights
        Commission and, 82
    see also civil rights movement
Alabama
    civil rights movement in,
        82–83, 85, 87–89
Alliance for Progress, 66, 77
Amagiri (Japanese destroyer),
    28–29
Anniston (Alabama), 83
Arabian Nights, The, 19
Arashi (Japanese destroyer), 28
Area Redevelopment Act, 78
Arlington National Cemetery,
    102
armed forces reserves
    ban on segregation in, 84
Arvad, Inga, 27
atomic bomb. See nuclear
    weapons
Auchincloss, Hugh D., 44

Ball, George, 68
Bartlett, Charles, 11, 43
Batista, Fulgencio, 60
Bay of Pigs incident, 60–62, 103
    see also Cuba, U.S. invasion of
Berlin, 63, 65, 66, 67, 73
Berlin Wall, 66
Bethlehem Steel, 15
Billings, LeMoyne K., 21, 22
Birmingham (Alabama)
    civil rights movement and,
        82, 87–89
Boston, 13–14
Boston Post, 42
Bouvier, Jacqueline Lee. See
    Kennedy, Jacqueline
Bouvier, John Vernon, III, 44

Bowen, Lester W., 33
Bradlee, Benjamin, 93
Buddhism, 76
Bulkey, George, 93
Bundy, McGeorge, 68
Burner, David, 70, 78, 95
Burns, James MacGregor, 12,
    28, 38, 41, 43, 44

Cambodia, 74
Camelot, 105
Campbell, Judith, 94
"Can a Catholic Become Vice
    President?" (Look magazine
    article), 50–51
Cape Canaveral (Florida), 80
Cape Kennedy (Florida), 80
Castro, Fidel, 60–62
Catholicism. See Roman
    Catholicism
Central Intelligence Agency
    (CIA)
    invasion of Cuba and, 60–61
Chamberlain, Neville, 24
China, 37, 63
Choate (school), 20–21, 23
CIA. See Central Intelligence
    Agency
civil rights bill, 89, 104–105
civil rights movement, 10
    demonstrations in
        Birmingham, Alabama,
        87–89
    Freedom Riders, 82–83
    Kennedy and, 89, 104–105
        addresses on, 86, 87, 89
        support for, 46, 59
    march on Washington, D.C.,
        89–90
    nonviolence and, 85
    Rosa Parks and, 85
    University of Alabama and,
        89
    U.S. Civil Rights Com-
        mission report on, 82
    voting rights and, 83
Cold War, 10
    Africa and, 68

Berlin and, 63, 65, 66, 67, 73
    Cuban missile crisis and,
        68–71
    Latin America and, 66–67
    nuclear test ban and, 71–74,
        103
    origins of, 63–64
    relations between Kennedy
        and Krushchev in, 64, 66,
        68
    Southeast Asia and, 74–76
Collier, Peter, 93
Commander Hotel, 41
communism, 10
    in China, 37, 63
    Cold War and, 63–64, 65,
        66–68, 72, 74
    Joe McCarthy and, 49–50
    Kennedy and, 72, 103
    as totalitarianism, 63–64
    see also Soviet Union
Congress of Racial Equality
    (CORE), 82–83
Connally, John, 97
Connally, Nellie, 97
CORE. See Congress of Racial
    Equality
cortisone, 40, 93
Cronkite, Walter, 101
Cuba
    missile crisis, 10, 68–71
    U.S. invasion of, 60–62
Curley, James, 32, 38
Cushing, Richard (cardinal),
    93
Czechoslovakia, 63

Dallas (Texas), 96, 97–98
debates, 57–59
democracy
    Kennedy's thesis on, 23–24
Democratic Party conventions
    of 1956, 50–51
    of 1960, 56–57
desegregation, 83, 84–85
desoxycorticosterone acetate, 39
Dien Bien Phu, 74
Dobrynin, Anatoly, 70

DOCA. *See* desoxycorticost-
erone acetate
Donovan, Robert J., 31
Dulles, Allen, 61
Duong Van Minh, 76

East Germany. *See* German
Democratic Republic
economic issues
Kennedy on
as president, 78, 79–80
as representative, 37–38
education
Kennedy's support of, 82
see also public schools
Eisenhower, Dwight D.
Cuba and, 60
economic growth under, 78
at Kennedy's inauguration,
59
space program and, 105
support for in Massachu-
setts, 42
electoral college, 46
Evans, Arthur Reginald, 30
ExComm. *See* Executive
Committee of the National
Security Council
Executive Committee of the
National Security Council
(ExComm), 68–69, 71

Farmer, James, 83
Federal Bureau of
Investigation
Kennedy's relationships and,
27, 94
Federal Republic of Germany,
63
Fitzgerald, John F. (grand-
father), 14, 32, 33
Fitzgerald, Rose. *See* Kennedy,
Rose
Food-for-Peace program, 67–68
foreign affairs
Alliance for Progress, 66, 77
Kennedy on, as
representative, 36–37
Peace Corps and, 68, 70
U.S. invasion of Cuba, 60–62
see also Cold War; South
Vietnam
Foreign Affairs (journal), 46

Fox, John, 42
France, 74, 75
Freedom Riders, 82–83

Gagarin, Yuri, 80
Gandhi, Mohandas, 85
Garfield, James, 100
Geneva Accords (on
Indochina), 74, 75
German Democratic Republic,
63, 66
Germany
British appeasement of, 23,
24
Cold War and, 63, 66
see also Berlin
Giancana, Sam, 94
Gilpatrick, Roswell, 93
Great Britain
appeasement of Nazi
Germany, 23, 24
Joseph P. Kennedy as
ambassador to, 22, 26

Hagikaze (Japanese destroyer),
28
Hartington, Billy, 30
*Hero for Our Time: An Intimate
Story of the Kennedy Years, A,*
(Martin), 65
Hersey, John, 34
Higher Education Act, 82
Hiroshima, 73
Hitler, Adolf, 23, 24
Ho Chi Minh, 74
Hood, James, 89
Hoover, J. Edgar, 27, 94
Horowitz, David, 93
Horton, Ralph, 21
"hot line," 73–74
housing, 35–36
Huber, Oscar, 97
Hue, 76
Humphrey, Hubert H., 53–54,
55–56
Hungary, 63

Indochina
France and, 74, 75
Geneva Accords and, 74
see also South Vietnam
Interstate Commerce
Commission

desegregation and, 83
Irish immigrants
in Boston, 13–14

*Jack: The Struggles of John F.
Kennedy* (Parmet), 40, 42
*JFK: The Presidency of John F.
Kennedy* (Parmet), 94
*John F. Kennedy and a New
Generation* (Burner), 70
John Kennedy (MacGregor), 44
John Kennedy, A Political Profile
(MacGregor), 18
Johnson, Lady Bird, 98
Johnson, Lyndon B., 53
Kennedy's assassination and,
96–97
Medicare and, 80
on Ngo Dinh Diem, 75
as vice presidential
candidate, 56
Vietnam War and, 104
Warren Commission and,
100

Kane, Joe, 33
Kefauver, Estes, 51
Kelley, Robert, 85
Kennedy (Sorenson), 48, 91
Kennedy, Caroline (daughter),
91–92, 102
Kennedy, Edward (brother),
33
Kennedy, Eunice (sister), 33,
35, 41
Kennedy, Jacqueline
Jack's assassination and, 97,
98
Jack's funeral and, 102
marriage to Jack, 43–44, 47,
93–94
Nikita Khrushchev and, 65
in presidential election of
1960, 54
Kennedy, Jean (sister), 33, 41
Kennedy, John, Jr. (son),
91–92, 102
Kennedy, John F.
assassination, 97–98
Kennedy's comments
preceding, 96–97
James Reston on, 105
birth, 13, 14

communism and, 72, 103
early life
    allowance request of, 18
    childhood homes, 16
    family life, 16–19
    family wealth and, 15
    illnesses in, 19–20, 21–22
education of, 20–22, 23, 27
as father, 91–93
health and ailments
    Addison's disease, 12, 22,
        39–40, 46, 91, 93
    back problems, 22, 27–28,
        30, 46, 48, 91, 93
    efforts to hide, 15, 20, 40
    improvements in, 91, 93
    during World War II,
        27–28, 30
    as a youth, 19–20, 21–22
Inga Arvad and, 27
Jim Curley and, 38
Joseph Kennedy and, 26,
    30–32, 33, 34, 42, 92, 94
journalistic career, 30
the Kennedy myth and, 15,
    20, 22, 30–31, 47, 105
liberalism and, 77–78, 79
marriage to Jackie, 43–44,
    47, 93–94
nicknamed "Ratface," 21
playboy image of, 39
political ability, 33–34
political career
    beginnings of, 30–32
    civil rights and, 46, 59
    as congressman, 34–38
    decision to run for the
        presidency, 52, 53
    Democratic convention of
        1956, 50–51
    Democratic convention of
        1960, 56–57
    first campaign of, 33–34,
        35
    Joe McCarthy and, 49–50
    presidential election of
        1960, 10–11, 57–59
    primary elections of 1960,
        52–56
    as senator, 44–46
    senatorial campaign of
        1952, 41–43
presidency, 10

Alliance for Progress, 66
Berlin and, 65, 66, 67, 73
civil rights bill, 89,
    104–105
civil rights issues, 84–85,
    86–87, 88–89
Cold War and, 63–68
economic policy, 78,
    79–80
education and, 82
Food-for-Peace program,
    67–68
inauguration, 59
invasion of Cuba, 60–62,
    103
Kennedy's happiness with,
    91
Kennedy's national
    popularity, 95–96
legacy of, 103–105
legislative failures in,
    78–80
military buildup and, 25,
    65–66
New Frontier theme,
    56–57
Peace Corps and, 68, 70
poor start of, 59–62
relations with Krushchev,
    64, 66, 68
Robert Kennedy and, 15
Southeast Asia and, 74
South Vietnam and, 75,
    76, 103–104
space program, 80–82,
    105
State of the Union mes-
    sages, 63, 78, 79–80
tax cut proposals, 79–80,
    104–105
Profiles in Courage, 48–49
public image of, 10–11, 12,
    47
Roman Catholicism and, 10,
    50–51, 54–55
on Rose Kennedy, 17
siblings, 14
Why England Slept, 23, 24–27
in World War II
    awarded Navy and Marine
        Corps medal, 30
    enlistment in Navy, 27, 28
    PT 109 and, 24, 27–30, 31

Kennedy, Joseph, Jr. (brother),
    14, 41
    childhood relationship with
        Jack, 19
    death of, 30
Kennedy, Joseph P. (father),
    10, 13
    business career, 15–16
    Democratic convention of
        1956 and, 51
    education of children, 20–21
    family life, 16–17
    Jack's allowance request, 18
    Jack's entry into politics and,
        30–32
    Jack's political career and,
        33, 34, 42
    on Korea, 37
    marriage to Rose Fitzgerald,
        14
    political career, 22–23, 26
    publication of Why England
        Slept, 26
    relationship with Jack, 94
    stroke of, 92
Kennedy, Kathleen (sister), 30,
    39, 41
Kennedy, Pat (great-
    grandfather), 13–14
Kennedy, Pat (sister), 33, 41
Kennedy, Patrick Bouvier
    (son), 92–93
Kennedy, Patrick Joseph
    (grandfather), 14
Kennedy, Robert (brother)
    as attorney general, 15, 61
    civil rights and, 83, 84, 88
    Cuban missile crisis and, 68,
        71, 103
    investigation of labor
        unions, 46, 77
    on Jack's health, 12
    in Jack's political campaigns,
        33, 41
    Joe McCarthy and, 50
    Martin Luther King Jr. and,
        59
Kennedy, Rose (mother), 13
    family life and, 16–17
    on Jack's health in
        childhood, 19
    on Jack's military enlistment,
        28

in Jack's political campaigns, 33, 41
marriage to Joseph Kennedy, 14
Kennedy, Rosemary (sister), 12, 15
Kennedy myth
 Camelot and, 105
 development of, 15, 105
 of Jack and Jackie's marriage, 47
 on Jack's entry into politics, 30–31
 on Jack's health, 15, 20, 22
The Kennedys (Collier and Horowitz), 93
Khrushchev, Nikita, 83
 Cuban missile crisis, 68–71
 Jacqueline Kennedy and, 65
 nuclear test ban and, 71–72
 relations with Kennedy, 64, 66, 68
King, A. D., 89
King, Coretta, 59
King, Martin Luther, Jr.
 arrest of, 59
 demonstrations in Birmingham, Alabama, 87
 "I have a dream" speech, 89–90
 nonviolence and, 85
King Arthur, 105
King Arthur and His Knights, 19
Knebel, Fletcher, 50

Labor Rackets Committee, 46
labor unions, 46, 77
Laos, 74–75
Laski, Harold, 26–27
Lasky, Victor, 39
Latin America, 66–67
Lee, Janet, 44
Liberal Party, 79
Limited Nuclear Test Ban Treaty, 71–73, 103
Lincoln, Abraham, 100, 103
literacy tests, 83
Lodge, Henry Cabot, Jr., 41, 43, 76
London School of Economics, 21–22
Look (magazine), 50
Luce, Henry, 26

MacGregor, James, 18
Making of the President, The, (White), 58
Malone, Vivian, 89
Manchester, William, 35, 83
Mao Tse-tung, 63
Martin, Ralph G., 65
Mazo, Earl, 59
McCarthy, Joe, 49–50
McCone, John, 68
McCormack, John, 38
McKinley, William, 100
McLaughlin, Edward, 34
McMahon, Patrick, 29–30, 31
McNamara, Robert, 68
Medicare, 79, 80
Meredith, James, 85–87
military. *See* armed forces reserves
Mississippi, 85–87
Monroe, Marilyn, 94
Montgomery (Alabama)
 civil rights movement and, 82, 85
Moody, Sidney C., Jr., 23, 51, 91
"Muckers Club," 21

Naru Island, 30
Nazi Germany. *See* Germany
Neville, Michael, 33
New Frontier, 56–57
New Yorker
 Hersey article on PT, 34, 109
Ngo Dinh Diem, 75–76
Ngo Dinh Nhu, 76
Nhu, Madame, 76
Nixon, Richard M., 11, 34
 television debates of 1960, 57–59
nonviolence, 85
Norris, George, 48
North Vietnam
 creation of, 74
 efforts to overthrow Ngo Dinh Diem, 75
nuclear weapons
 ban on testing, 71–74
 U.S. and Soviet testing of, 66

O'Connell, William (cardinal), 14

One Brief Shining Moment: Remembering Kennedy (Manchester), 35, 83
O'Neill, Thomas P., 34
Oswald, Lee Harvey, 98–100, 101

Parks, Rosa, 85
Parmet, Herbert S., 22, 27, 40, 42, 49, 94
Pathet Lao, 74
patrol torpedo boats. *See* PT 109
Peace Corps, 68, 70
Pearson, Drew, 48–49
Plum Pudding Island, 29, 31
Poland, 63
poll taxes, 83
Powers, Dave, 34, 42, 48
President Kennedy: Profile of Power (Reeves), 20, 53, 76, 96
President's Committee on Equal Employment Opportunity, 85
Princeton, 22
Profiles in Courage (Kennedy), 10, 11, 48–49
PT 109, 24, 27–30, 31
PT 109: John F. Kennedy in World War II (Donovan), 31
public schools, 84

Question of Character: A Life of John F. Kennedy, A (Reeves), 22, 28, 47, 94

Reader's Digest
 Hersey article on PT 109, 34
Reeves, Richard, 20, 53, 76, 88, 96
Reeves, Thomas C., 22, 28, 47, 94
Reston, James, 52
Roman Catholicism
 Kennedy's political career and, 10, 50–51, 54–55
Roosevelt, Franklin D., 59
 Joseph P. Kennedy and, 22–23, 26
Roosevelt, Theodore, 19
Roper, Elmo, 59
Ross, George, 30
Rostow, Walt, 75

Ruby, Jack, 99, 101
Rusk, Dean, 68, 70

Schlesinger, Arthur M., Jr., 40
  Camelot myth and, 105
  on Kennedy's Addison's
    disease, 40
  on Kennedy's entry into
    politics, 31–32
schools. *See* public schools
SCLC. *See* Southern Christian
  Leadership Conference
Securities and Exchange
  Commission, 22, 23
Shepard, Alan, 80
Shigure (Japanese destroyer),
  28
Smith, Al, 54
Sorenson, Theodore, 50, 91
  authorship of *Profiles in
    Courage* and, 48–49
  Camelot myth and, 105
  Cuban missile crisis and, 68
  hired by Kennedy, 45
  on Kennedy's growth as
    president, 103
Southeast Asia
  Cold War and, 74–76
  see also South Vietnam;
    Vietnam War
Southern Christian Leadership
  Conference (SCLC), 85
South Vietnam
  creation of, 74
  Kennedy's plans for,
    103–104
  reign of Ngo Dinh Diem,
    75–76
Soviet Union, 10
  Cold War and, 63, 64, 66
  Cuban missile crisis, 68–71
  nuclear test ban, 71–74
  space program of, 80
  U.S. racial problems and,
    83–84
  U.S. wheat sales to, 74

space exploration, 80–82, 105
St. John, Seymour, 23
St. Lawrence Seaway, 45
St. Matthew's Cathedral, 102
Stanford University, 27
Stevenson, Adlai, 51, 53
supply-side economics, 80
Supreme Court, 84, 85
Symington, Stuart, 53

Taft, Robert A., 48
taxes
  Kennedy's proposals for,
    79–80, 104–105
  see also poll taxes
Taylor, Maxwell
  Cuban missile crisis and, 68
  South Vietnam and, 75
teas, 41–42, 43
television
  in 1952 campaign, 42
  coverage of Kennedy's
    assassination and funeral,
    101–102
  Kennedy's use of as
    president, 95–96
  presidential debates of 1960,
    57–59
Texas
  Kennedy's assassination in
    Dallas, 97–98
  Kennedy's campaign trip to,
    96
Thich Quang Duc, 76
Thompson, James, 97
*Thousand Days: John F. Kennedy
  in the White House, A,*
  (Schlesinger), 40
"Tip" O'Neill. *See* O'Neill,
  Thomas P.
Tippit, J.D., 98, 100
totalitarianism
  communism as, 63–64
  Kennedy's thesis on, 23–24
Trade Expansion Act, 78
Triumph and Tragedy: The Story

of the Kennedys (Moody), 23,
  39, 51, 91–92, 95
Truman, Harry S., 37, 66
Tse-tung, Mao. *See* Mao Tse-
  tung
Tuscaloosa (Alabama), 89
Twenty-Fourth Amendment, 83

unions. *See* labor unions
United States government
  ban on segregation in, 84–85
  Civil Rights Commission, 82
  Maritime Commission, 22
University of Alabama, 89
University of Mississippi
  civil rights movement and,
    85–87

Vietcong, 75
Vietnam, 74, 75–76
Vietnam War
  Lyndon Johnson and, 104
  origins of, 75–76
voting rights, 83

Wallace, George, 89
Warren Commission, 100
Washington, D.C.
  civil rights march of 1963,
    89–90
Washington Times-Herald, 44
Watkins, Arthur, 50
Webster, Daniel, 48
West Berlin. *See* Berlin
West Germany. *See* Federal
  Republic of Germany
West Virginia, 54–56
wheat
  U.S. sales to Russia, 74
White, Theodore H., 58, 105
Why England Slept (Kennedy),
  23–27, 65
World War II
  Kennedy in, 24, 27–30, 31
  origins of, Kennedy on, 23,
    24–25

Picture Credits

Cover Photo: John F. Kennedy Library

Archive Photos, 50, 75, 102

John F. Kennedy Library, 11, 13, 14, 15, 16, 17, 18, 19, 21, 26, 29, 32, 36, 37, 43, 45, 48, 53, 56, 60, 64, 72, 73, 77, 92, 95

Library of Congress, 54, 69, 80, 84, 87, 88, 90, 104

Lyndon B. Johnson Library, 99

National Archives, 57, 62, 98, 100

About the Author

Michael V. Uschan has written six books, including *The Importance of John F. Kennedy; A Basic Guide to Luge,* part of a series written for the U.S. Olympic Committee; and two of the books in Lucent's A Cultural History of the United States Through the Decades series pertaining to the 1910s and the 1940s. Mr. Uschan began his career as a writer and editor with United Press International, a wire service that provided news reports to newspapers, radio, and television. Because journalism is sometimes called "history in a hurry," he considers writing history books a natural extension of the skills he developed as a journalist. Mr. Uschan has also worked as an editor, writer, and public relations specialist for the Hawaii Department of Education and Wisconsin Department of Public Instruction. He and his wife, Barbara, live in Franklin, Wisconsin, a suburb of Milwaukee.